"Why Did You Do That?"

Other Tyndale—AACC books

Family Shock: Keeping Families Strong in the Midst of Earthshaking Change
by Gary R. Collins, Ph.D.

Intimate Allies: Rediscovering God's Design for Marriage and Becoming Soul Mates for Life
by Dan B. Allender, Ph.D., and
Tremper Longman III, Ph.D.

High-Maintenance Relationships: How to Handle Impossible People
by Les Parrott III, Ph.D.

Psychology, Theology, and Spirituality in Christian Counseling
by Mark R. McMinn, Ph.D.

Counseling Children through the World of Play
by Daniel Sweeney, Ph.D.

"WHY DID YOU DO THAT?"

Understand Why Your Family Members Act As They Do

WM. LEE CARTER, Ed.D.

Tyndale House Publishers, Inc.
WHEATON, ILLINOIS

The American Association of Christian Counselors is an organization of professional, pastoral, and lay counselors committed to the promotion of excellence and unity in Christian Counseling. The AACC provides conferences, software, video and audio resources, two professional journals, and a resource review, as well as other publications and resources. Membership is open to anyone who writes for information: AACC, P.O. Box 739, Forest, VA 24551.

Designed by Melinda Schumacher
Edited by Lynn Vanderzalm

Library of Congress Cataloging-in-Publication Data

Carter, Wm. Lee.
    Why did you do that? : understand why your family members act as
they do / Wm. Lee Carter.
      p. cm.
    ISBN 0-8423-7174-5 (softcover : alk. paper)
    1. Family—United States—Psychological aspects. 2. Communication
in the family—United States. 3. Behavioral assessment—United States.
4. Family—Religious life—United States. I. Title.
HQ536.C385 1996
306.85—dc20   96-520

Printed in the United States of America

03 02 01 00 99 98 97 96
8   7   6   5   4   3   2   1

CONTENTS

Introduction

Part One—Look Before You Speak
    1. Observe Your Family's Behavior *3*
    2. Listen between the Lines *29*
    3. What Are You Really Trying to Tell Me? *63*

Part Two—Understand Your Family's Patterns
    4. Rigidity: Refusing to Budge *93*
    5. Dependence: Struggling for Independence *111*
    6. Argumentativeness: Winning at All Cost *131*
    7. Withdrawal: Playing It Safe *149*
    8. Indulgence: Taking All That Life Offers *165*

Part Three—Respond Rather Than React
    9. Who's in Control of the Family? *191*
    10. Value Each Other *221*

Part Four—Set the Tone for Family Growth
    11. Learn to Communicate *245*
    12. Strong Marriage, Strong Family *279*

About the Author *289*

INTRODUCTION

Sue Carrel looks her eight-year-old son in the eye.
"Jeremy, yesterday you told me that you did not take
money from my purse. Yet when I washed your jeans
today, I found a five-dollar bill in your pocket. That's
the amount that was missing from my purse. I think
you lied to me. Why did you do that?"

Not waiting for his son to reply, Jeff Carrel raises his
voice and asserts, "Jeremy, you are grounded for a week.
I will not tolerate that kind of behavior. You know better than that."

Sue, startled by her husband's quick outburst, won-
ders, *Why did Jeff do that? Why couldn't he at least have
let Jeremy try to explain?*

Oblivious to the situation between her parents and her
brother, fifteen-year-old Tracy waltzes into the room and
walks to the refrigerator. Sue notices the fresh coat of pur-
ple nail polish on Tracy's fingernails and lets out an exasperated sigh. *Why must this child always push the limit? Why
does she wear that garish nail polish? She knows we don't like it.*

But rather than make an issue of the nail polish, Sue
shakes her head, withdraws to the dining room, and
starts to set the table.

• • • •

Many of us are like Sue Carrel. We observe our family
members' behavior and ask, "Why did my son do

that?" "Why did my spouse react with such rigidity?"
"Why did my daughter do that?" "Why did I withdraw
or lose my temper or undercut my spouse's authority?"
Sometimes we ask the questions in exasperation; other
times we are curious. Still other times we are genuinely
concerned about a family member's behavior.

Why are such questions even important? Why do we
need to know why people act as they do?

I believe that family conflict results when we *react*
rather than *respond* to each other's behavior. My years as
a psychologist and family counselor have convinced me
that if we learn to understand the message and emotions
behind our family members' behavior, we will be able to
respond to that underlying message rather than react to
the behavior. The results will be closer relationships,
deeper understanding of each other, and family growth.

This book is designed to help you move from reacting to responding, from conflict to harmony. Part 1 will
help you learn to observe your family members' behavior and listen between the lines so that you can understand the message behind the behavior. Part 2 will give
you tools for understanding how common family
behavioral patterns—rigidity, dependence, argumentativeness, withdrawal, and indulgence—can cause conflict. Part 3 explores the issues of power, control,
self-esteem, and valuing each family member. Part 4
sets the tone for family growth by examining the
dynamics of effective communication and how a strong
marriage is an essential foundation for a stable, healthy
family. At the end of each chapter you will find a "Family Notes" section designed to help you reflect on your
family, gain insight from Scripture, and set some goals
that will result in your family's growth.

Before we launch into the book, I would like to share some thoughts about the nature and composition of our families.

WHAT IS A FAMILY?

We can find no single definition of what a family is. But we can be certain about several things. A family functions as a unit, a whole. No one family member best characterizes the family. Each person is a spoke in the family wheel. As each family member relates to the others, the family takes on definition.

For example, the marriage relationship is the foremost relationship in the family. From it, all others derive. When pain is experienced in marriage, all other family members suffer. In addition, each parent and child have a relationship, be it healthy or dysfunctional. Parent-child relationships often provide a barometer of how the family as a whole is functioning. Finally, siblings relate to one another. Siblings may unite to shield themselves from the hurt of a broken marriage relationship. They may push the family apart and be the catalyst for marital conflict.

What makes a family function smoothly? From my experience in my childhood family, my present family, and my years of observing families in the counseling office, I have identified three essential ingredients of a happy family: leadership, unity, and the ability to embrace change.

A Family Has Leaders

There is no such thing as a family without leadership. Parents are ordained to be family leaders as they fill the roles of teacher, guide, authority figure, role model, decision maker, expert, or manager. The parent as leader is a well-ingrained thought in Christian teaching. At times we parents take the position of leadership and create a character not intended for family life: tyrant, potentate, ruler, or any other term synonymous with power. At other times we allow this position to depreciate to unnecessary weakness: fall guy, scapegoat, wimp, or other designations of powerlessness.

Leadership requires a balance between dominance and inadequacy. The following ten guidelines help us keep balance in the position of family leaders:

1. An effective leader welcomes alternative points of view.
2. The leader is a teacher, whether the lessons are positive or negative.
3. A leader's actions speak louder than his or her words.
4. A strong relationship is often the best form of influence.
5. Wisdom is best gained through experience rather than word.
6. Decisions should take into account individual strengths and weaknesses.
7. Consistency leads to trust in relationships.
8. Followers interpret a leader's indecision as a decision.
9. Flexibility is a strength, not a weakness.
10. Every person, regardless of age or experience, is capable of change.

A Family Is a Unit

Through the ages, people have grown in their understanding of how the family functions. Today's family experts recognize that a family is not a group of individuals who happen to live together. A family is a single unit. Call it an organization or a clan or a tribe or a team—our language includes many words that embrace the concept of the family as a unit.

Not only is each family member a part of a unique unit, but each member is a valuable part of the unit. In biblical days, women and children were offered diminutive roles in the family unit. Jesus no doubt turned many heads when he invited the little children to sit on his lap (Matthew 19:14). Decades later Paul created a similar stir when he expressed that "husbands ought to love their wives as their own bodies. He who loves his wife loves himself" (Ephesians 5:28). We Christians have a tendency to compartmentalize family relationships, even though people like Christ and the apostle Paul challenged us to be radical as we profile relationships within the family. They enlightened us to the fact that family means unity. As you shape your family into an effective unit, remember these ten guidelines:

1. Every member makes an equal contribution to the family.
2. Family relations are fused by embracing, touching, and pleasant facial expressions.
3. The need for love and affection is as basic as the need for air and water.
4. The differences of each member make a family distinct.
5. Family members differ in their roles but not in their personal value.
6. Equality, not superiority, should be each family member's goal.

7. A family is a community; each member should be a good neighbor.
8. Though family members cannot give equally, all should give something.
9. When a family works together, God is more clearly understood.
10. Family life is a partnership, not "me versus you."

A Family Changes

I've done it with my family, and I suspect you have too. We have sat together and browsed through old photographs. Like Tevye in *Fiddler on the Roof*, I don't remember growing older. But there in living color, and even in black and white, is proof that I have changed.

Change is a potentially frightening word. I believe that fear of change is what compels many families to fall apart. By sticking with whatever used to work, by believing what we have always believed, and by doing it the way our parents did it, families stagnate. Not that constancy is a bad thing; lack of tradition or precedent or regularity can tear a family apart too. As in all of life, balance is the key to successful family life. The past must be balanced against the future. What has been must be reconciled with what will be. As life moves, so must the family. As you experience change within your family, remember these ten guidelines:

1. By exploring the world together, family members find it easier to venture further.
2. Everything done today will resurface sometime tomorrow; therefore, do it right the first time.

3. Always be who you are; deception never works in the end.
4. Family success is measured not by accomplishments but by relationships.
5. Emotional and spiritual growth flourish in a world of love.
6. Every time we seem to have found the answer, new truths appear.
7. Age makes no difference in the need to adjust and change.
8. None of us will reach perfection, but we should all keep trying.
9. The real struggles in life are not with others but within ourselves.
10. No family member can ever earn the love of another. It must be a gift.

I pray that as you read this book, you and your family will grow in your ability to understand and respond to each other. I can't do that for you, but I hope that my skills as a family counselor will

• *encourage you,* perhaps for the very first time, to look at your family in an honest way. As this book helps you treat each other with dignity, you can learn to trust yourself and others.

• *give direction* to your family's confusion. This book will help you understand how your family functions and the unique dynamics in your family.

• *provide objectivity* to family relationships. Family members' personal views of things may keep them stuck in a frustrating rut. By helping you see discrepancies that can be corrected, this book can give you a richer perspective of family life. Family members can see how they look to others.

• *remind you of your value* as individuals. This book will demonstrate how to show attention to individual differences as a way of reminding family members that they have worth.

• *offer a model* of how to solve problems that affect the home. As you read the many dialogues, case studies, situations, and alternative responses in this book, you will grow in your ability to practice patience, understanding, tolerance, concern, and balance.

• *provide a glimpse of God* as you search for his perfect will for your family's life. As you implement the principles outlined in this book to address family conflict, you will see God's character—love, patience, forgiveness, grace, mercy, truth—in fresh ways in your family.

Please know that even though I cannot personally meet each of you who read this book, you are in my prayers as I write these words. I trust that God will guide your family, even as he does mine.

PART ONE
Look Before You Speak

CHAPTER ONE

Observe Your Family's Behavior

"**I** WAS going to come in and take the dishes out of the dishwasher as soon as we were through with our game. Mom had already told me that I had to be in by seven o'clock, and I was going to be. The way I figured it, I could come when she told me and then empty the dishes. Why did she get mad at me? I feel as if I have to do everything the moment she says it. Why can't I decide when to do it—as long as I get it done? She thinks I won't do my chores unless she's standing there watching me. Good grief! What does she think I am anyway?"

"She doesn't understand that what I'm doing is for her good. She should have learned by now that every time she breaks the rules, especially as blatantly as she did, she's going to be punished. I dread the arguments we have afterward. I try to explain that if I just let her do what she wants, when she wants, she'll never learn

3

to be responsible. She says she doesn't want to learn about manners or responsibility or stupid things like that. She claims her friends act the same way she does. Well, I don't care who acts that way. *My* child won't if I have anything to do about it!"

Do these responses sound familiar? The first was obviously made by a peeved child complaining that her mother does not understand her. She was upset because she wanted to do things one way while her mother had a different idea in mind. The second was registered by her agitated mother. She was explaining the reasoning behind her behavior. She had the child's best interests in mind, even though she and her daughter clearly disagreed. Outwardly, it seemed that this parent and child agreed on nothing. Actually, they were in agreement on one matter: *Each felt misunderstood!*

THERE IS A REASON FOR EVERY BEHAVIOR

Struggling to understand each other's behavior is common for family members. How often have you heard the following sentiment expressed in your house? "Why did you do that? I just don't understand you!" Parents say that about children who persist in their wayward behavior—in spite of the fact that the parents are well read on the topic of parenting. Children, in turn, make the same complaint against their parents. They wish adults would quit interfering in their lives. Spouses who are struggling to keep the family together question each other. One family member may feel that the other is undermining efforts to give order to family life. So, struggles for understanding emerge.

Every family member, from the youngest to the oldest, wants to be understood. Infants hold nothing back when they scream for attention. Unschooled in the art of tact, they let loose with all that is in them just to point out a simple need—a diaper needs to be changed or hunger needs to be satisfied. As infants grow through childhood, into adolescence, and eventually into adulthood, those screams do not disappear. They simply take on different forms.

Have you ever been with an adult whose "cry" sounded remarkably like an overgrown baby's cry? I have. You probably have too. We all can identify with the basic human desire for understanding.

Why family members act as they do is a question that has teased the brain of many family authorities. Depending on the experts' school of thought, their answers may vary. Some claim that the unique constellation of the family heavily influences the behavior of its members. Others emphasize that behavior is merely a reaction to the events in the household. Still others believe that the family's ability or inability to function is dependent on the family background of each parent.

In my work with families, I have seen several factors that influence behavior. Listed below are principles I rely on to interpret family behavior:

1. When words are inadequate, people find alternate ways to express what they feel.
2. Behavior is a communication device. Our actions *do* speak more loudly than our words.
3. The events that precede and follow a communication have a direct bearing on future communication.
4. Family members develop unique communication styles that fit their temperaments.

5. Communication barriers go up when people misunderstand each other.
6. A family member's interpretation of events involves developmental factors, experience, personality tendencies, and personal history.
7. Societal, cultural, and gender differences encourage differences in the way males and females as well as children and adults communicate with one another.

Communication is a complex process, and it's easy for us to miss what another person is really trying to say because we have misunderstood his or her words and actions. The following excerpt from a family counseling session illustrates how family members can be easily confused by the real meaning beneath behavior. In this scenario, the parents are trying to come to grips with the behavior of their son, Kevin.

CASE STUDY: KEVIN, THE REBELLIOUS TEENAGER

Father: I thought things were going pretty well around here until you pulled a stunt like that. Did you honestly think that you could get away with slipping out the bedroom window? Is shooting firecrackers under other people's windows more fun than sleeping? Do you realize what you're doing to our family? You're tearing us apart!

Kevin: Hey, don't blame everything on me! Maybe I did something I shouldn't have, but you and Mom have been yelling at each other a lot more than usual lately. How do you think that makes me feel? You've got to admit that this family is going downhill because of the way you talk down to everyone. It's not all *my* fault the whole family is mad, you know.

Mother: Kevin's right, Harry. You have been acting like a tyrant. I'm almost afraid to say anything at all to you because you may explode. It's gotten to the point that I feel as if I'm walking on eggshells around you all the time.

Father: And I suppose that's why you've been giving me the silent treatment the last few days. You won't talk to me or touch me or even let me sleep on the same side of the bed with you!

Mother: Harry!

Counselor: I guess the big question is which of you has done something wrong. Maybe no one has done anything wrong in this family. *(pause)* Don't misunderstand. I'm not saying I think it's right for Kevin to sneak out of the house to create mischief in the neighborhood. And I don't think it's the right thing for a father to level his family verbally or for a wife to give her husband the silent treatment. I suspect each of you would agree with me.

Father: I can agree with you, but I'll tell you this: I won't tolerate it when a boy as young as he is *(pointing to Kevin)* does the things he does.

Counselor: I think we would be wise to take a closer look at each family member's behavior to find the *reason* each of you acted as you did. Maybe all of you were sending an important message through the way you acted. Kevin, can you give your parents any good reasons for what you did?

Kevin (shrugging): I can give you some excuses, but I don't know if I can give any real answers. I just did what I did to see if I could have some fun.

Counselor: I don't know if you realize it, Kevin, but you just gave us some valuable information.

Kevin: Like what?

Counselor: By saying you just wanted to have fun, you suggested you don't like rules and that you wanted to see if you could do what *you* wanted to do and not what someone else thought you should do. You wanted to be the exception to the rule.

Kevin: I'm also getting tired of being grounded all the time, so I figured I might as well try to get away with whatever I could so I could have a little fun.

Counselor (to father): I'm sure you don't mean to come across to your family as a man who gripes and complains constantly, but there must be a reason why you would raise your voice. I suspect it has something to do with being dissatisfied with the way things have been going at home.

Father: I just can't tell you how much I want this family to pull together. I want more than anything to let Kevin have fun with his friends, but I can't let him get away with shooting firecrackers under people's windows late at night. That's not right. *(turning to his wife)* I love Gina, but it hurts my feelings when she won't tell me what she's thinking. I know I don't always act as if I love her, but I don't know what else to do. I'm sure I do gripe and yell a lot more than I should.

Mother: When I don't talk, it's not that I want to withdraw from the whole family. I just feel lost to know what else to do or say to make things better. Sometimes it seems that I'm doing everybody a favor to go off by myself. I'm afraid if I don't, I might explode.

Counselor: I would imagine that when you're quiet, there's a lot of anger underneath all that silence.

IMPORTANT MESSAGES LIE BENEATH FAMILY ARGUMENTS

What had started out as a family argument ended in a healthy discussion of the messages each family member attempted to convey through behavior. By the end of the hour, each family member had a more thorough understanding of the others.

Only a small percentage of family communication is verbal. Experts in the field tell us that as much as 90 percent of what we communicate is conveyed through behavior. Obviously, for families to get along, they must pay close attention to each family member's behavior. Through behavior, family members give many clues about their real thoughts and feelings.

By his actions, Kevin communicated a desire for greater freedom in making choices—a reasonable desire. His dad indicated through his griping and yelling that he was concerned about his family and wanted them to pull together as a unit—a worthwhile goal. Kevin's mom withdrew to express her fear that her family would continue to decline—a very real possibility. None of these family members' thoughts and emotions were *wrong*. Perhaps their communication was skewed, but each underlying message was worth consideration. Their problem was that they became bogged down in their communication. None of them felt understood.

Family members become mired in frustration when they react negatively to negative behavior. They assume that someone's negative behavior was done intentionally to cause harm. Certainly, a son may purposely go beyond normal adolescent mischief, a husband may hurl words meant to sting, or a wife may intentionally stonewall her husband by remaining silent.

Families become stuck when they are unable to dig deeply enough to find the messages beneath their outward pain. Notice how the behaviors in the following vignettes express deeper, underlying messages.

• Several months after a serious automobile wreck, a distraught woman confessed that she had actually caused the accident because she had wanted to die. "I was afraid to kill myself, but I thought that if I died in an automobile accident, I could get rid of my emotional pain and could die in a way that wouldn't disgrace my family."

• In a rare moment of introspection, a man accused of physically abusing his children admitted, "I know I treat

my kids badly. I was treated even worse when I was a
boy. Sometimes when I'm whipping one of my own children, I feel as if I'm actually beating my father the way
he used to beat me. You may say I'm crazy, but I almost
look forward to spanking the kids for that reason."

• A fourteen-year-old girl, who just days earlier had
discovered that she was pregnant, broke down in tears
as she said, "I feel I can never face my friends again.
What will they say to me when they find out I'm pregnant? I'm supposed to be this wonderful Christian girl
who doesn't do anything wrong, and now I've got to
admit I'm no better than anyone else." Looking up, she
said, "But the only time I feel loved is when I'm with
my boyfriend. My parents are so strict. I'm not sure
they even care about me."

• A twenty-year-old college-age girl struggling with
an eating disorder said, "You just can't believe my life
history. If I told you what my family life has been like,
you'd think I had been reading too many novels. About
the only thing I have any control over is how I look.
My family has practically ruined how I feel on the
inside, so I want to do all I can to make myself look
good on the outside."

Now, how would you respond—not react—to these
people? What if these people were your family members? How would you respond?

The first step in a healthy response is to enter the
other person's emotional world. While that may seem
threatening to you, it is one of the most helpful things
you can do. Invariably, when parents as family leaders
can picture themselves *acting, feeling,* and *thinking* as
the other person would, family relationships change.
They come alive. After observing, interpreting, and

responding to the message behind the behavior, parents can lead the family to richer, deeper levels of understanding.

Try to picture how these people will feel when they hear the following responses from another family member.

> *To the distraught woman:* It would humiliate you to say that life hurts so bad you want to end it all. You want us to know how bad you feel, but you don't want us to hurt the way you hurt.

> *To the abusive father:* I don't think anyone really knows the burden you carry from your own childhood. Wouldn't it be nice to be able to put the past behind? But it keeps haunting you.

> *To the pregnant teenager:* People look at you and think one thing. But when you look at yourself, you see something completely different. There are a lot of confusing feelings running through you right now. You're running on empty.

> *To the young person with an eating disorder:* Somehow life has gotten away from you. It seems that nothing can convince you that you're worthwhile. We try, but it's not good enough. I'm concerned about your eating habits. You're concerned about things that are much more serious than that.

How would these people respond? Certainly they would feel more understood. People who feel understood are more likely to express deeper emotions, feelings they may have hidden from others for years. The offer of an understanding response helps family members look beyond problems to solutions. The helping family member diffuses potential struggles for control within the family. *When families shift their focus from inappropriate acts to underlying messages, change can occur.*

EACH FAMILY MEMBER HAS A DIFFERENT UNDERSTANDING OF THE FAMILY

Another tool family leaders will need to discern messages behind behavior is an understanding of each family member's personality, position in the life cycle, and life experience. Accurately perceiving family members' thoughts and feelings involves discerning both the overt and hidden messages being communicated. For example, the look in a child's eye may suggest hurt, anger, embarrassment, irritation, or any of a number of emotions. Her behavior may demand immediate attention, or it may tell you that you can deal with the feeling later. Through her tone of voice, the child may be asking for a hug or suggesting that her parents keep their distance.

Family Members' Personalities

Family members' personalities influence the way they perceive others. Each of us is born with a personality. With that personality comes a predisposition to see things according to that personality's prominent emotions. Those emotions color our sensitivity to life's events. Differences in personality may result in behavioral clashes and emotional friction.

Situation: A family's six-year-old son has thrown a temper tantrum, a common situation. A fight between the

13

boy and his father started when the boy hit his father because his father had said no to the boy. After the father's efforts to calm his son failed, he spanked the boy. The child is now in his room crying. A pall has been cast on the home atmosphere.

Boy's perception: The child feels he has been treated unjustly. He sees no reason why his dad couldn't have given him what he wanted. He thinks his parents are mean. Anger, venomous anger, surges through him toward his father. As he lies in his room crying, he vows that he will continue to push his father. His strong will compels him to fight back.

Father's perception: An anxious man, the father is unnerved. He feels completely helpless to do anything about his son's tantrums. He worries that his son will grow up to be a juvenile delinquent. The father had a brother who acted just like this son, creating a living nightmare for the family. The father's emotions are so strong that he literally feels sick. He is upset with himself for losing his cool and with his son for being so relentlessly stubborn.

Analysis: The boy has a take-charge, controlling personality. It is his practice to test limits, forcefully state his feelings and opinions, and coerce others into surrender. His father is a more passive man who prefers to talk matters out. He prefers reasoning with others rather than engaging in verbal warfare. The son, though he is only six years old, recognizes his father's anguish when the adult is forced to exercise parental discipline. The child's resolve to fight back is based on his conviction that he can eventually wear down his dad's emotions. If the father can recognize his son's forceful behavior as a by-product of a strong personality, he will be better equipped to deal more objectively with future struggles.

Position in the Life Cycle

A family member's stage in life also plays a major role in the way that person perceives his or her world. A five-year-old child, a teenager, a young adult, and a fifty-year-old adult will interpret life from their vantage point of youth or maturity. Adults are often impatient with children and adolescents because of their lack of wisdom and judgment. Teenagers, on the other hand, may resent the way their parents treat them, making them feel immature and incapable of making independent choices. Family leaders can ease conflict by becoming aware of each family member's position in life.

Situation: At age fourteen, Linda is in love—at least that's what she says. Her boyfriend is three years older than she is and is every bit as enamored with Linda as she is with him. Linda cannot understand her parents' unwillingness to let her date this boy. She admits she is young to be dating, but she feels more mature than most of her friends. She believes her parents are wrong to put tight restrictions on her social activities. Linda and her parents have just had another in what has become a series of wrangles about this topic.

Linda's perception: Linda believes her parents are living in the Dark Ages. She is offended when her parents claim to know what she is experiencing. She believes her parents' youth was worlds different from hers.

When her parents tell her they are acting in her best interests, she mocks them, saying, "If you were doing what is best for me, you would get off my back and give me some freedom."

Parents' perception: Linda's parents agonize over how to get through to their daughter. She has never been the rebellious type, but for the first time she openly challenges their leadership in the home. They try to reason with her, but it does no good. Both stay upset because they fear an emotional chasm is splitting them from their daughter. They worry that they will not be able to bridge the gap that currently separates them.

Analysis: Linda's immature, adolescent reasoning convinces her that she can make independent decisions about boyfriends. Her inexperience at life fails to warn her of the potential pitfalls of dating an older boy at such a young age. Linda's parents are further down life's road and have seen too many girls get hurt by early romantic affairs. They are convinced that their decision to hold tightly to their convictions is the right one. By recognizing that Linda's naïveté in relationships will inevitably result in disagreement, they can avoid needless arguments with their daughter. After all, she will not comprehend their logic until she is several years older.

Life Experience

Two people who are at the same stage in life and have similar personalities may still view situations very differently. What makes the difference is their life experience. This factor is especially important in a family setting in which family members react out of their own experiences. Family members will interpret a circumstance based on how it uniquely affects them.

Situation: Brenda is a single mother doing the best she can to raise her only son, John, age ten. She divorced seven years ago. John's father used to visit the boy regularly and kept him several weeks each summer. The dad remarried four years ago. Since that time, John has seen his dad only a few times. The last time John spent an extended visit with his dad was two summers ago. The father and son now communicate only by phone, and that is usually initiated by the boy. John complains regularly about his dad. Brenda tells him that he just has to learn to live with the fact that his daddy is worthless.

Mother's perception: Brenda was abused by her former husband and still bears the emotional scars of those dreadful encounters. At times she sees her former husband's behavior in her son and fights herself to keep from despising John as she does his father. She is bitter that the man will not fulfill his parental obligations, but she feels silent pleasure that John doesn't have much to do with his father anymore. She doesn't talk about the man any more than is necessary and is irritated when John mentions his name.

Son's perception: John feels abandoned by his father. That rejection has caused him to question his own value as a person. In his way of thinking, a boy must not be valuable if his father chooses another woman and her children over him. He wants to talk to his mother about his feelings, but he feels he can't. He believes it is best simply to keep his thoughts to himself because no one can be trusted.

Analysis: Even though John is angry with his father—just as his mother is—the man is still his father. John hopes beyond all hope that maybe his dad will become the father he needs. John's mother has lost her affection for her former husband. In her mind, John would be better off without the man. As difficult as it is, her best approach with John is to encourage the boy to be open with his feelings. He needs help sorting out his emotions. Eventually he must decide for himself the role he wants his father to play in his life.

In a growing family, the family leader not only must accurately perceive each family member's feelings but also must become an advocate for each family member. It does the family little good to tally a scorecard to decide which family member is right. Family life deteriorates further when the leaders take sides, causing others to feel alienated. The adult's role is to perceive the underlying message behind the behavior, be an advocate for other family members, and provide an atmosphere in which the family can decide how they will respond to a personal need. Like an artist, the family leader must deftly sidestep struggles for control. By perceiving the unique views of others, family members can open up communication, allowing productive changes to occur.

Take note in the following case study of how each family member approaches life differently. By helping family members correctly perceive each other's needs, the counselor set the stage for positive change.

CASE STUDY: REGGIE CONCEALS HIS FEELINGS

Eight-year-old Reggie sat next to his mother in my office. Mrs. Hemphill had asked that he be included in our session. "Reggie and I are having a problem. Whatever you tell me to do, I want him to hear it. We're going to decide right now how to handle this mess."

I looked at Reggie and could detect his disgust. He had obviously been blamed for the rift that currently separated him from his mother. Mrs. Hemphill wore a look of determination. She had been through the wringer with her son and was ready to get off the roller coaster they had been riding the past few days.

"Let's take a look at the problem. Something has obviously gotten between the two of you."

Mrs. Hemphill glared at Reggie, signaling that she intended to divulge all the details of their disagreement. "Reggie refuses to go visit his dad. He says that the last time he was there, his stepmother played favorites with her daughter, so he says he's never going back. I say he has to go. I tried to tell him I didn't like the woman either, but that doesn't mean he can stay home when the judge says he has to go. Reggie said he would do whatever you say. That's why we're both in here today."

"I didn't say I wasn't going," Reggie rebutted.

"You most certainly did! Don't you sit in here and lie to me like that. You tell Dr. Carter what you told me!" Reggie crossed his arms over his slight chest, a sure sign that his lips were momentarily sealed. "Go on. Tell him!"

Stone silence.

Reggie had control over his mother right then and did not intend to relinquish his position. Disgustedly, Mrs. Hemphill looked at me and explained, "Reggie told me that the judge is nothing more than a fat pig who's being paid off by his daddy. He says if the judge wants him to go visit his daddy, he can come and get him."

"I don't mind seeing Daddy. It's *her* I don't want to see. I *hate* her."

"You can't say that, Reggie. You don't hate anybody!" his mother warned.

"I hate *her.*"

Reggie looked out the window, avoiding his mother's cold glare. Mrs. Hemphill took her gaze off her son and shifted her eyes toward me. It was obviously my turn to speak.

"Reggie," I said, drawing the boy's eyes toward me, "you and your mother are both feeling pretty miserable right now. You're worried that she might not be taking you seriously when you say you don't want to be around your stepmother."

"She wants me to like her."

"Your mother wants you to like your stepmother? Huh. You would've thought it would be the other way around."

"I hate the way she treats her daughter and the way she treats me."

"Can you explain?"

"She treats Candice nice, but she doesn't like me."

"And that makes you feel left out. You'd like what Candice gets."

"My daddy treats her nice too."

"I see. When you're with your daddy, you want his attention. You don't want him to give so much attention to Candice. You want him to spend his time with you."

"So what am I supposed to do?" interrupted Mrs. Hemphill.

"You're in a quandary," I responded. "If you force Reggie to go to his father's house, it's as if you're turning your back on your son. But if you let him stay home, you're violating his father's rights."

"And besides, Reggie needs to see his daddy. I just wish his daddy would spend more time with him. If he only knew how much that would mean to Reggie . . ." Mrs. Hemphill's voice trailed off. The few seconds of silence that followed seemed to last minutes.

"When Reggie tells you he won't go to his daddy's house, you feel desperate. It's hard to know which way to go. Should you give in to Reggie's wish but face the wrath of his father? Or should you send Reggie to his daddy's, knowing that he doesn't want to be there? Neither solution makes you feel comfortable."

This time it was Reggie who butted into the conversation. "I'll go." His mother looked at him with disbelief. Silently she thought that he was being cruel to her. If he was willing to go to his father's house, why had he put her through the agony they had experienced the past few days?

I leaned forward in my chair and quietly said to Reggie, "You love your daddy. It would mean the world to you if you had more time with him."

"Yes, sir," Reggie said, barely able to push his words through his trembling lower lip.

••••

As the session continued, the emphasis shifted from Reggie's refusal to visit his father to his wavering self-esteem. He made it plain that the issue was not over

21

visitation rights. The real issue was not even his dislike for his stepmother. His need was to feel secure. As I responded to Reggie and his mother, I emphasized each family member's perception of the problem. As their respective views were drawn into the open, problems seemed to resolve themselves. Mrs. Hemphill had entered the session with the idea that I would tell them the answer to their dilemma. In the end, Reggie had offered the solution. Once that was taken care of, we were able to shift our attention to Reggie's real need, his hunger for affirmation.

By focusing on other family members' perceptions of a problem, families are able to dig deeper into the trouble surrounding them. When family members believe that they have an advocate, they are more likely to express their real concerns, not just surface matters. That advocate need not be a family counselor. What happens in a counselor's office can often be transferred to the home. Understanding that each family member sees life differently helps parents take control of the home atmosphere; barriers are removed, creating opportunities for growth.

SELF-UNDERSTANDING PROMOTES UNDERSTANDING OF OTHER FAMILY MEMBERS

Another essential tool to understanding your family is understanding your own strengths and weaknesses. Read the following set of statements. Respond to each statement. Afterward study your responses to guide you as you decide how you can most effectively relate to your spouse and children. (1 means not at all; 2 means sometimes; 3 means most of the time.)

1 2 3 I tend to be goal oriented in the things I do.

1 2 3 I am patient.

1 2 3 I am a pensive and reflective person.

1 2 3 People often describe me as bubbly and outgoing.

1 2 3 Ambiguity bothers me. I have a strong need for closure.

1 2 3 It is very important to me that other people like me.

1 2 3 I can be critical of others if the situation calls for it.

1 2 3 I don't like to talk about really sticky subjects, like sex.

1 2 3 I am easily irritated by people who won't help themselves.

1 2 3 I need to know what others expect of me.

1 2 3 I tend to be protective of others, especially the underdog.

1 2 3 Pushy people really get under my skin.

1 2 3 Confrontation makes me feel uncomfortable.

1 2 3 I tend to try to fix people's problems.

1 2 3 I say things based on how it may affect my reputation.

1 2 3 I can make friends with just about anyone.

1 2 3 I usually keep my personal feelings to myself.

1 2 3 I can effectively handle a busy schedule.

1 2 3 I tend to take on more responsibilities than I can handle.

1 2 3 I tend to bare my feelings to others.

After you have responded to the statements, review your answers. Try to detect a pattern in your answers. Ask yourself these questions:

- Will my family respond to me as a caring, concerned person, or do I place too much emphasis on results?
- Am I sufficiently expressive of my personal views? not expressive enough? too expressive?
- How skilled am I at keeping the focus on my family's needs and off my own agenda?
- Do I have the staying power to stick with family members through thick and thin?
- How strongly do I show my personal views? Is that good or bad?
- Do I have the ability to be flexible as the situation warrants?
- How objective am I in dealing with my spouse and children?

Your understanding of yourself should include personal values, goals, spiritual beliefs, emotional tendencies, as well as likes and dislikes. If you wonder what to do with the personal strengths and flaws this exercise has uncovered, I encourage you to use the strengths to move your family toward growth and use the weaknesses as stepping-stones to self-improvement. Family leaders are not perfect. Just like everybody else, we need to improve.

SET THE TONE

Family leaders set the tone for the kind of communication that takes place in the home. As you respond rather than react to family members' behavior, they in turn can learn to perceive one another's emotions. Remember, look before you speak. Before you react to a family member's behavior, look beyond the behavior to the underlying message and the underlying emotions. Try to use statements that bring emotions into focus and that encourage family members to search for the deeper meanings beneath words and actions. When helping other family members understand emotions more completely, use statements similar to these:

- "I know how irritating it is to come home from work only to find the kids fussing at each other over trivial matters. It's enough to make you want to scream."
- "After we argue, I get an empty feeling inside. I feel so lonely. I guess you do too."
- "It seems that there are no easy solutions. It's frustrating, isn't it?"
- "You want so badly for me and Mom to understand you, but it's hard to know how to put your feelings into words. Sometimes you reach the point that you want to scream. Your feelings can be that strong."
- "It's difficult to understand how a boy can be that uncaring toward you. It makes you want to strike back to let him know how you feel."
- "When you think back on how things were just a few years ago, you wonder how we even made it through all we've experienced."

Summary: When our family members display confusing behavior, we react: we sometimes accuse, jump to conclusions, yell, withdraw, punish, or collapse in frustration. Often our reactions cause conflict. We can take the first step to avoiding or resolving family conflict if we learn to look before we speak. This chapter has discussed the importance of observing family members and trying to hear the message behind their behavior, taking into account family members' personalities, stage in life, and life experience.

The next chapter will take us another important step: learning to listen between the lines, learning to express understanding so that our family members will open up to us and reveal the motives behind their behavior.

1. As you study your own family, pay close attention to the behavior of each family member. What personal insights can you gain from the way each person chooses to act? How aware is each family member of the others' emotional needs? Ask your family to respond to these same questions.

2. At some point in the next day or two, ask one of your family members to help you identify what he or she is trying to convey through behavior. Do you recognize some qualities that your family members are unable to see? How are family members' messages obscured by their behavior?

3. Brainstorm with your family about ways you can more effectively tell each other what you feel. What behaviors could replace those that are ineffective or destructive? How can your family use verbal communication to strengthen the way the family acts?

4. Discuss with your family whether it is good or bad to show others your feelings through your behavior. You will probably find out a lot about the way your family communicates. From your discussion, generate goals for change.

5. To understand adequately how a family member feels, try to "become" that person, even if only for a

brief time. Try to understand that person's frame of reference, even though your own life experiences will create interference.

6. Try out your perceptions. When you think you understand what the other person is trying to communicate, communicate your perceptions to the other person. Then ask for feedback. Are your perceptions accurate? Remember, though, that the goal is not for you to be right but for your reflective statements to help your family member open up to you.

CHAPTER TWO

Listen between the Lines

GREG'S face bore a look of guilt. He had done something wrong, and try as he might, his expression would not allow him to hide his crime. His lips were clasped shut, bound by an oath of silence. It did not matter, though, because his face screamed, "I'm guilty! I did it!" As if he were looking at himself in a mirror and could clearly witness his own silent confession, Greg knew that he had become his own worst enemy. Inwardly he thought, *If I could just get rid of this shameful look, I could pull this one off. I could convince my mother that I didn't do what she thinks I did.* His cheeks and eyelids began to burn with the fire that sears a condemned child. He hated that sensation.

"Greg, why did you do that?"

"I don't know."

"Yes, you do know. Don't give me that answer. I

demand that you tell me! Why did you lie to your brother?"

Greg's eyes dropped straight to the floor as if he might find an acceptable answer lying there. There was none. Slowly allowing his gaze to drift as high as his mother's waist, he offered what seemed to be the best response. With a slight shrug and without opening his mouth, he intoned, "I don't know."

"Oh, Greg. Can't you do better than that? How many times do I have to tell you that if you constantly lie to others, they'll never believe you when you tell the truth? Do you want your name smeared like that? Do you want people to think of you as a liar?"

Greg's lip turned downward. He had not heard much of what his mother had said. He simply knew that she was mad at him—again. It seemed that she was always mad at him. With just a slight shake of his head, he gestured his answer to his mother. It was not good enough to prevent the guilty verdict and the sentence that followed.

"You can just plan on staying in for the rest of the day. If you can't tell the truth to your own family, I see no reason to let you just walk out of here and do what-ever you wish. You can stay in for the rest of the eve-ning and think about what we've just discussed. Go on to your room."

WHY THE FAMILY SHOULD ASK WHY
Why did you do that? As we discuss family relationships, we find ourselves continually returning to this baffling question. This concern has confronted every family since Day One. Adam probably asked Eve why she bit into the forbidden fruit. Adam and Eve no doubt asked

their son Cain to account for his heinous act against Abel.

Beneath this question is a healthy implication: *If you can tell me why you did what you did, perhaps we can find a way to repair a wrong.* Why, then, do family members so consistently sidestep such a helpful question? If the aim of the questioning person is to help, it would follow that the respondent would happily provide a full explanation.

But most family conversations don't work that way.

As I noted in the previous chapter, the majority of communication is nonverbal. Remember, fully 90 percent of what we communicate is through means other than the spoken word. What we do, the emotions we show, the messages we insinuate—all these things play a more important role in family communication than the words that pass from our lips. Comprehending this fact is fairly simple. Accurately interpreting family behavior is often complex and difficult.

Greg had probably lied to his brother in order to maintain some semblance of power over him. Or perhaps he enjoyed watching his brother whine in frustration. Or maybe he hoped to cover up a wrongdoing that he knew would result in stern punishment. Or maybe he had all of these motives. Greg's mother, on the other hand, wanted to correct him so that he could restore his wounded relationship with his sibling. She wanted to teach him a valuable lesson about life so he could be happy and contented with himself.

So what prevented Greg from answering his mother's question and learning from her disciplinary action? When his mother focused so strongly on his wrong behavior, Greg no longer felt free to express his real motive or feelings. He felt attacked. He became defensive, guarding against a potential onslaught of guilt and judgment. So Greg responds, "I don't know." What he really is saying is, "I know why I lied to my brother, but I don't want to tell you because I know you will punish me and make my life miserable."

How can Greg's mother help him open up and tell her why he did what he did? My experience as a family counselor has taught me that family members will reveal their true feelings if they are confident the other person will understand them, respect their feelings, and be trustworthy. As family leaders, we must take the lead in establishing an environment in which our family members will feel safe to open up. As we discuss how we can create that environment, keep in mind that the most important question is not, What must I *do* to show my family I understand them? but What *personal characteristics must I develop* so that my family will know that I understand them? Let's look at three qualities family leaders must develop in order for them to lead their family into growth.

I Understand You

Nothing feels better than to be understood. Without understanding, change cannot take place. If a parent is deficient in other areas but has worked toward understanding, progress can still be seen in hurting families. Too often parents feel a sense of urgency to solve the family's problem. But before we can give direction to family needs, we must demonstrate understanding.

How can we communicate to our family members that we understand them? Let's look at some questions several of my clients have asked *before* they decided to open up to their family members.

- Do they view me with any prejudices or preconceived ideas?
- Are they interested in me as an individual?
- Can they possibly think the way I think?
- Will they judge me by what I say or the way I act?
- Are they able to remain objective about our family's problem?
- Do they set aside their own opinions so they can comprehend mine?
- Can I trust them to keep my comments confidential?
- Do they threaten or intimidate me with their knowledge?
- Will I be allowed to form my own conclusions, or will they force their thoughts on me?

If your family members asked these questions about you, how would you measure up? Or look at it another way. Think about people whom you feel offer you understanding. What is it about those people that communicates understanding? Clients have offered these responses:

- "It's as if he became me while I was talking."
- "She didn't tell me I shouldn't feel that way."
- "I didn't even have to explain my feelings. He knew what I meant."
- "I started talking, and she listened. It felt so good. I kept talking."
- "I couldn't believe that he was so calm when I

told him what I felt. I loved it. It felt so comfortable."

- "I felt understood, and for the first time I think I began to understand myself."
- "She didn't say much, but I know she knew what I meant. She wanted to hear more."

CASE STUDY: HUSBAND AND WIFE EXPRESS UNDERSTANDING
In the following excerpt from a dialogue between a concerned couple, notice the role understanding plays in their family dynamics.

Husband: You look bothered. What's wrong?

Wife: It's Brittany. Honestly, I think she's the one who runs our house. I don't know what to do with her. She's . . . well, she's just different. You know what I mean.

Husband: Yeah. Hard to believe she's just eight years old, isn't it?

Wife: I keep telling myself that. You know, we knew something was different about her even when she was a baby. She wasn't like the other two. Remember how she never wanted us to cuddle her?

Husband: And she's been throwing temper tantrums since she was six months old. She doesn't lie on the floor and kick like she used to, but she sure is a tiger.

Wife: I'm never sure if we're handling her the right way. I hate it that we all stay torn up because of that one child.

Husband: Children like Brittany are hard to figure out. Makes you wonder what went wrong. Makes me wonder too.

Wife: Maybe it's something we've done to make her be this way. But then, I read in books and magazines that some children are born with a difficult personality. I never thought we'd have a genuine strong-willed child living in our home. It's exasperating.

Husband: I think about it too. I hate it when we fight about how to handle her. Kind of makes me mad at Brittany for coming between us like that.

Wife: Sometimes the fights are bad. I hate them too.

Husband: We need relief, don't we? You're tired of fighting, and so am I.

• • • •

Notice several things about this exchange. Neither spouse attempted to analyze or interpret family communication patterns. They could save that for a later time. Neither directed blame toward the other or toward the absent child. This couple succeeded in maintaining neutrality. Their sole aim was to step inside each other's shoes to try to comprehend their mutual family struggle. Both left the conversation feeling hopeful that they could work out a solution to their family problem. Understanding does that to a couple. It leaves them with a sense of hope.

I Respect You

A theme that will be sounded throughout this book is that all of us want to feel in control of our corner of the world. As family leaders, parents should help other family members experience that sense of control. The adults must believe that each member of the family can deal constructively with whatever problem confronts him or her. The parents' role is to guide the family as it adjusts to life's changing tide. Respect for other family members is often shown silently by comments that are *avoided*. Often what we *fail* to say is more important than what we actually speak. The family leader need not provide a quick answer to all the dilemmas that confront the home. Consider the following contrasting comments and their potential effect on the family member involved.

> *Teenager:* Dad thinks he knows everything. I can't say anything without him giving his opinion. He tries to tell me how to think, how to feel, how to act. I can't stand the way he pushes himself on me.

> *Mother's harmful response:* But what if Dad is right? Maybe he's just trying to help you.

> *Teen's interpretation:* It's no easier getting through to my mom than it is getting through to Dad.

> *Mother's helpful response:* It hurts to feel that Dad doesn't understand you any better than he does. You wonder what it takes to get through.

Teen's interpretation: I can trust my feelings to my mom. She lets me say what I feel.

••••

Wife: I've tried to tell Theo that there are more important things than watching television. I want him to be more involved with the rest of us.

Husband's harmful response: He wouldn't listen anyway. He'd just start a fight with you if you tried to get him to change.

Wife's interpretation: He thinks the situation is just as hopeless as I do.

Husband's helpful response: I'm sure you've stretched your brain thinking of what can be done to change things. I agree. It *would* be a real treat to have Theo join the family.

Wife's interpretation: Maybe the two of us can come up with some options for dealing with this problem.

••••

Young child: I don't care what happens to me. That was the last time Peter's going to get away with what he did to me.

Parent's harmful response: When I get through punishing you, I'll bet you'll wish you hadn't hit Peter.

Child's interpretation: She thinks Peter was right, just like everybody else does.

Parent's helpful response: You felt so strongly about what Peter had done, you wanted everybody to know what you felt.

Child's interpretation: She's different. She doesn't tell me I'm bad.

• • • •

Showing respect to other family members increases their sense of being understood. Respect suggests that no attempt will be made to keep the other person from being exactly who he or she is at that very moment, bad feelings and all. Respect says, "I believe that you can learn from your experiences." Through this response, family leaders send a message that they are involved and committed to the family. Their response demonstrates their belief that if they let family members experience the full range of their thoughts and feelings, they have a greater chance of making positive changes. When family members perceive that we respect them, they will often be more open to our opinions and direction.

You Can Trust Me

Family members often find it hard to be honest with each other. One reason is simply that many of us find it difficult to talk about our personal feelings. Another reason is that we are afraid of how the other person will react. Children are afraid to talk to their parents about personal matters because they fear they may be punished for admitting doing something wrong. Or a spouse may be hesitant to discuss strong feelings because those feelings may be taken the wrong way.

There is little that I have not heard about family relationships in my office. I do not blush easily when I hear of a family member's indiscretions. I have learned to deal with the intimate details of how people relate to one another. It's the nature of my profession. Yet once I cross the threshold of my house, I change roles. I become a father and husband rather than a counselor. My wife and daughters need to be convinced that they can trust me with their feelings.

It is not at all uncommon to hear family members stammer as they say, "This is extremely hard for me to tell you, but . . ." A task of the family leader is to put other family members at ease as they discuss the most personal aspects of their lives. In an atmosphere where trust can be found, change occurs.

CASE STUDY: THE SON LEARNS THE TRUTH ABOUT HIS DAD
Listen as one mother successfully deals with her son's awkward, tangled web of emotions:

> *Mother:* This has been a hard week, hasn't it? A week is a long time when you're dealing with tough things.

> *Son:* Tell me about it. Why did Dad do that? How could he do those things with that woman? Doesn't he realize what he's doing to the rest of us? Why did he tell me about it anyway?

> *Mother:* I think he knew you were going to find out eventually, and I guess he assumed you'd rather find out from him than from someone else. There

was too much talking among Dad's family once they all found out. Grandmother is so mad that she's about ready to divorce her own son. (pause) So how are you doing after all of this week's happenings? I can only imagine that you've got all sorts of feelings running through you.

Son (almost in tears): I don't know what I feel. This has been one of the worst weeks of my entire life.

Mother: I'm sure it has. We've all had a hard week. Even your dad.

Son: Those feelings just won't go away. I'm so mad at Dad, I wish he'd just drop dead. Why did he do that?

Mother: What's running through your mind? You probably have some jumbled emotions.

Son: I'm confused. I really don't know what to think.

Mother: I'll bet. I feel broken up and confused too. It's hard to make any sense of the whole situation. It hurts a boy to hear that his dad has made a mistake. You probably wonder what's going to happen between me and your dad.

Son: Mm-hm.

Mother: Robert, what your dad did happened two years ago. I had a feeling it was going on. When I found out, I wasn't really surprised. Part of me wants to kill him, and part of me wants to be understanding. We're not going to get a divorce over this. At least I don't think we will. But since all of this has come out during the last few days, it has forced us to deal with some things we would rather not deal with. It's one thing for me to be upset, but I hate to see you so upset.

Son: I've cried so much in the last week, I wonder if I have any tears left.

Mother: Robert, you used the word *confused* a moment ago. Confusion can mean a lot of things. What do you mean when you say you're confused?

Son (head hanging): I just don't know. I feel all kinds of things. I don't feel so sorry for Dad. Maybe I feel sorry for you. Some for Dad, I guess. I don't know.

Mother: Robert, I know you hate being drawn into these kinds of problems.

Son: Who wouldn't?

Mother: I just want you to know that whatever you feel, you can come to me anytime you need to. We're all struggling. I'm angry with Dad just as you are, but I'm trying to make sense of this mess. Come talk to me whenever you feel like it.

••••

The conversation between this mother and son wound down with each person wading through confusion. Both had a unique set of emotions needing to be untangled. Yet recognizing her role as family leader, this mother set aside her own bitterness so she could respond to her son's emotional needs.

The mother successfully brought her son's emotions to the forefront. The sensitive nature of her comments sent a message of trust. She could be trusted to uphold his need for dignity. She could be trusted to identify his confusion accurately. The young man believed his mom could be trusted to walk him through a painful maze of feelings. In time, trust could help the family move slowly to a point of healing.

Family leaders show trust when they send this message: *Whatever situation we find ourselves in, I will count all your thoughts and emotions as valid.* Robert felt anger, resentment, even hatred. These emotions could become unhealthy if they are allowed to grow and fester. In her trusting way, his mother showed acceptance, affection, and compassion. Her message, "You can trust me with your feelings," gave rise to her son's positive nature. Trust yields hope. Bolstered by his mother's trust, Robert has a good chance of growing through a difficult experience.

LEARN FROM CHRIST'S WAY OF
UNDERSTANDING OTHERS

In my favorite Scripture passage, John 8:1-11, Jesus encountered an adulterous woman. He expressed to her a tenderness that strikes at my heart each time I read it.

Jesus set an atmosphere that put the woman at ease.
Like any person confronted with an intimate and
embarrassing flaw, she waited for Jesus' reaction to her
sin. He quickly observed her need and responded by
being the person who could coax her from despair to
contentment. His actions surprised the woman and her
accusers. He refused to condemn her, although we can
guess that she was fully aware that he did not condone
her behavior. He did not look down on her as other
people did. Instead, he gave her understanding. He
showed respect for her person. He made himself a target for her trust. Though Scripture does not tell us what
happened to the woman after this encounter, most
scholars suspect she changed for the better. Some
believe she became a devoted follower of Christ.

Christ's acts remind us that *our character is more important than our behavior* as we try to foster understanding
in our homes. Note the contrast between Christ's
response and the behavior of the religious leaders who
brought the adulteress to Jesus. The teachers and Phari-
sees were judgmental, condemning, calloused, deceitful, spiteful, and inconsiderate. In contrast, Jesus was
calm, forgiving, accepting, tender, inviting, and considerate.

The personal characteristics parents bring into a
home are perhaps the most effective tools they have
for helping their families grow. As God's love shows
through family members, hearts open to receive forgiveness and healing. Within the context of a healing environment, growth occurs. Family members learn about
themselves, about each other, and about effective ways
to deal with change.

DRIFT FROM ONE WORLD TO ANOTHER

If family members are to grow, they need an understanding response from each other. It seems that to understand a child or spouse would not be so difficult. I was once seven years old. So were you. I have lived through adolescence, as have you. When I look back on those years, I have many recollections of what it was like to be a child, a gawky preteen, and a teenager. We all have those memories.

Funny thing, though. Our children often assume that we do not know what it is like to live life from their perspective. You may have had a conversation like this:

Mother: Kenneth, I'm punishing you only because it's for your own good. When a boy throws eggs at a car and ruins the paint on it, he needs to be punished. I don't know what you were thinking when you turned that little trick, but it wasn't cute. You may not realize it now, but the lesson I'm trying to teach you is one you'll need down the road. I'm not your enemy. I'm just helping you.

Son: Mom, how can you know what I'm going to need years from now? Besides, my friends and I are going to pay for what we did. That's punishment enough. I don't see why you have to make me stay away from Gary's house for six weeks. You hardly even know what it's like to be me.

Mother: Yes, I do. Don't forget that I was your age once. I know exactly what you're going through. That's why I don't want you to make any more mistakes than you have to. I've made plenty of mistakes myself, and I don't want you to go through the same struggles I did.

Son: Mom, wake up! This isn't the sixties. Things are different from when you were a kid. What you learned back then may not apply to me. I doubt that you've ever thrown an egg at anybody in your whole life. You've probably never done anything fun in your entire life! I *know* what's best for me, and punishment isn't the answer.

Mother: Maybe you think you know what's best for you. I'm just trying to tell you to quit acting up so much. People won't think much of you if you don't learn to think before you act. I know you boys were just having fun, but look at where it got you.

Son: Who cares where it got me? What I'm saying is that I *don't* need to be punished, and you *don't* understand what I need.

• • • •

Conversations like this can and, unfortunately, often do go on endlessly without resolution. The typical result is that one or both family members leave the verbal exchange more frustrated than when it started. The probable outcome of the conversation between Kenneth and his mother is that Kenneth will repeatedly try to force his feelings and opinions on his mother. Even though the mother clearly showed care and concern, her focus on her son's misbehavior widened the gap between them. Convinced that she does not understand him, the boy will feel pushed to restate his opinions in a way that will get through to her. His stubbornness will swell in spite of his mother's attempt to communicate that she understands what he did and that she holds no judgment against him.

Kenneth's mother lost sight of the fact that the parent is the leader in the healthy family. She forgot that one of the most effective parental leadership skills is to look *beyond* the behavior to the underlying message. *Behavior represents a window to the emotions inside another person.* When we emphasize the behavior, we see only the surface. When we take the effort to look at the feelings and emotions beneath the behavior, family relationships move forward because family members feel understood. Consider the following example of how parental leadership can tighten family ties:

> *Mother:* You're not especially happy that I had to punish you tonight, are you, Kenneth?

> *Son:* No. I don't think you know what's best for me. I don't think you should've punished me at all. I've already learned my lesson.

> *Mother:* I can look back on when I was your age and remember going through the same feelings you're going through right now. You and your friends were having fun and didn't intend to make anyone mad. Now you feel helpless because someone else is making decisions that affect you and you disagree with what's being done.

Son: How can you know what it feels like? You've never thrown eggs at anyone before. You've probably never had fun in your entire life. This isn't the sixties anymore.

Mother: No, it's not. And you're right. I've never thrown an egg at anyone. The circumstances you face are different from what I've faced in the past. I'm simply saying that the feelings you have are the same as those I've had. No one likes to be punished, especially when you disagree with the punishment.

Son: Well, I know how we can fix that one. Don't punish me. Just let me pay my part of the damage, and then the whole ordeal is over. Then I won't be mad, and you can be satisfied that you've gotten your message across.

Mother: A world without punishment would be the perfect world. We'd all like that.

Son: There is no such thing as a perfect world. Believe me, I know.

Mother: You mean your world isn't what you wish it was?

Son: Not really.

Mother: Then tell me what you think. What would your perfect world be like?

Son: Well, for starters, I wouldn't let parents go around punishing their kids all the time.

Mother: That's the worst part of being a parent.

Son: What is?

Mother: Having to punish your kids. I don't enjoy seeing you get upset any more than you enjoy being upset. I can only hope that what I do makes a mark on you.

Son: Oh, it's making a mark on me, all right. It's not the right kind, though. Maybe you could just let me off.

Mother: That's another hard thing about being a mother.

Son: What's that?

Mother: Sticking with a punishment even though you know your child doesn't agree with you. But that's a part of my role—to do what I can to help you figure out what you need to do to be all you can be.

Son: Does this mean you're going to go easy on me?

Mother: What it means is that I understand what you're going through. Maybe I don't agree with what you did, but I'm trying to understand how you feel.

••••

The probable outcome of this conversation is markedly different from the first. Although the son had done something wrong, the mother successfully kept the focus of their conversation away from his misdeed. Showing understanding, respect, and trust did not mean she abandoned her role as a family disciplinarian. She did what she had to do. Instead of simply emphasizing his wrong behavior, though, she zeroed in on the feelings beneath his behavior. She also recognized that by pouting, her son was sending further messages, and she responded to his unspoken communication.

The mother felt no urge to argue with her son over whether or not his behavior was right. She felt constrained to insist that he rid himself of his negative attitude toward her. Even though she may not have convinced him that he should act differently, she *did* win a piece of his heart. She showed that she was more keenly interested in his personal needs than his outward behavior.

USE UNDERSTANDING TO DIAGNOSE FAMILY NEEDS

Responding to family problems is a daily activity. Even while you focus on one dilemma, other areas of concern surface. For example, while grappling with the problem of a child's persistent stubbornness, parents may realize that they are contributing to that problem by being quarrelsome with each other. As family members dig deeper into troublesome issues, they will uncover new concerns.

Often, family members take a shotgun approach to

solving family problems, trying to hit as many trouble spots as possible all at one time. It's better to focus on one problem area at a time. Honing in on a single issue will often allow deeper, more fundamental problems to come into focus. By following a line of thought through to its completion, you will see new issues emerge, as shown in the following situation.

A family consisting of a mother, a stepfather, a fourteen-year-old son, and a nine-year-old daughter is together in the family room. The daughter doesn't want to go to school. She frequently complains of feeling sick. Her mother thinks she is feigning illness but is never sure whether to be firm or soft in handling the girl. The stepfather feels helpless in dealing with the situation. He thinks the girl should be forced to attend school, sick or not. He feels powerless, however, because he is not the child's natural father. The brother constantly complains about the family's discord and says he wants to move in with his father, even though he is not emotionally close to his dad.

> *Mother:* How am I supposed to know if Ginny is sick or not? She looks and sounds really bad when she tells me what's wrong with her. But whenever she goes to school, the teacher always says she's fine.

> *Stepfather:* That's because she was never sick in the first place. She just wants your attention, so she says she's sick and then she gets to stay home with you. It's that simple.

Daughter: Uh-uh! I am sick. You don't know how much my stomach hurts when I get up in the morning.

Stepfather: Okay, maybe you're really sick, but you sure do get over it quickly. You need to quit missing school so much. You can't keep your grades up if you miss school.

Mother: But that's just it. She makes good grades. I figure that as long as her grades are up, it doesn't hurt for her to miss sometimes, especially if she truly seems to be sick.

Stepfather: I would agree, *if* I believed she was really sick, which I have yet to be convinced of.

• • • •

Thus far in the conversation, the family is focusing on a single problem: the daughter's illness. Obviously, the two adults disagree over the validity of the child's physical condition. For the parents to bring about effective change in the home, they will need to shift gears. Rather than focus on their own interpretation of their child's complaints, they should place themselves in their daughter's shoes, thinking as she does. Perhaps the girl is having thoughts like these:

- I'm scared of school. I hate doing anything new. Can't my mother see that?
- I don't know why I get sick. I just want to be told that everything is going to be all right with me.
- I hate to see my family fight so much. It makes

me feel guilty. On the other hand, they're fighting about me, which means I'm getting attention.
- What does my brother think about me? What about my parents? Are they getting tired of me? I feel so alone!
- I'm worried about what's going to happen next. Nothing good ever happens to me.

As hard as it is to leave one's personal mind-set, it is tremendously valuable to move into the other person's world. Until the parents can see the problem from their daughter's point of view, they will not understand the underlying message. Watch how the conversation progresses when the mother recognizes that her daughter needs understanding.

• • • •

Mother: Ginny, when children are sick, different feelings run through them. What feelings run through you when you're sick?

Daughter: I don't know. I just feel sick. I hate school.

Mother: It's not your favorite place to be?

Daughter: No. I'd rather be home.

Mother: Oh? Why's that?

Daughter: Because you're here.

Mother: And that keeps you from feeling sick?

Daughter: Yes. I feel fine when I'm at home.

••••

The daughter has now provided useful diagnostic information. She has confirmed that her sick feelings are most probably not due to a physical disorder. She may have a stomachache, but it is likely a result of nervousness rather than sickness. Ginny has suggested that she is rewarded in some way by staying home with her mother. The most obvious reward is substituting the burden of her school studies with her mother's attention. But the family still has a problem. Something must be done to get Ginny to attend school regularly. As the stepfather shows understanding, he also becomes part of the solution rather than part of the problem.

> *Stepfather:* You see, Ginny says that being at home is better than attending school. She enjoys being close to you. That's what I mean when I say she wants your attention, but maybe there's more to this problem than that.

> *Mother:* Like what?

> *Stepfather:* I'm wondering if Ginny is afraid of something. *(turning toward Ginny)* Ginny, are you scared of anything at school? Are the teachers giving you too much pressure? How about the other kids? Are they bothering you?

> *Daughter:* I don't know. I just hate going. I like being here with Mom. I want her to teach me at home.

Mother: Ginny, I felt the same way when I was young. I hated to do anything I wasn't sure I could conquer. I know exactly what you're going through. As I got older, I was angry that no one in my childhood had helped me face my fears. To this day, I don't like to face new situations. I'm afraid the same thing could happen to you, and I don't want that.

• • • •

A new problem has now been diagnosed: The mother lives through the emotions of her daughter. Ginny knows that too. For that matter, so does the husband, although he may not comprehend the complexity of the emotional entanglement between his wife and her daughter. The brother probably knows something is wrong, but he prefers to avoid thinking about it. He would rather leave the home than get involved. Even though he has not been a part of the family's discussion, listening to the discussion is therapeutic to him.

GUIDE THE FAMILY TOWARD CHANGE
Once family leaders come to grips with the problems confronting the family, they are more likely to discover how to get out of a circular pattern of dysfunction. To focus solely on the identified behavioral problem, in this case the daughter's refusal to go to school, might result in the elimination of that problem in favor of a related problem. The girl may start attending school regularly, but she could demand that her mother indulge her in other ways. The parents need to pay attention to the hidden reinforcers that push problem behaviors along.

In this family's case, the parents wisely paid attention to the underlying factors that influenced Ginny's behavior.

> *Stepfather:* If we force Ginny to go to school whether or not she's sick, she may feel that you've abandoned her. But if we let things go on as they have been, she may become a fearful adult who fails to live up to her potential.

> *Mother:* That's where I have a problem. I don't know how far we should push her.

> *Stepfather (pauses):* Ginny, we don't always force you to do things you don't want to do. But your mom's afraid that when you grow up, you won't be as successful as you're capable of being.

> *Daughter:* I don't care about when I'm grown up. You shouldn't worry about that. That's a long way off.

> *Stepfather (to wife):* I say we do what's best for her for the future.

> *Mother:* Can't we do both? I just hate seeing her so upset, and I know that's exactly what will happen if we force her to go to school every single time she complains.

> *Stepfather:* But you just said it yourself that you wish your parents had stepped in and helped you face your fears when you were young.

Mother: I know. I just hate making these kinds of choices. *(pause)* But we have to, don't we?

••••

By continually opening themselves to the needs of their own family, these family members were able to conclude that today's events have an impact on tomorrow's behavior. The mother struggled to admit what she could see happening to her family. She realized, though, that by keeping her daughter from confronting her fears, she was prolonging, even intensifying, a problem. She did not want Ginny to repeat the self-defeating cycle in which she is still stuck. She concluded that she must decide how to carry out her role as family leader.

The stepfather in this family was initially trying to force the issue of Ginny's school refusal to a head. Yet by stepping outside his own opinions and thinking as both Ginny and his wife might think, he became a help rather than a burden. Once he had accomplished that goal, his wife was open to his opinion.

IMPLEMENT A THERAPEUTIC PLAN

As the conversation draws to an end, these family members want an answer to their immediate problem. Should they force Ginny to attend school or temporarily give in to her refusal? The parents realized they must confront the pressing problem of Ginny's school refusal. But because they had successfully diagnosed that the problem was connected to other family needs, they were capable of tackling that undesirable task. Had the parents stubbornly refused to budge from their own opinions and preferences, an ugly stalemate would have resulted. Instead, they could work toward a resolution.

> *Mother:* So what are we going to do? Are you saying we should make Ginny go to school even if she seems to be sick and has a fever and has thrown up?

> *Stepfather:* Well, just look at it like this. We know that Ginny's refusal to attend school is not the real problem. We need to help her control her fears, and going to school is just one of them.

> *Mother (to daughter):* Honey, we really don't have a choice other than to send you to school.

> *Daughter:* But, Mom!

> *Mother:* You don't have to like what we're doing. I'm going to call your teacher tomorrow and talk to her about helping us make things as positive as we can for you.

> *Stepfather:* Ginny, we understand that you prefer being with your mom. We want you to go to school as you're supposed to, but we also need to make sure you get the kind of attention you need. We'll be sure to do that.

••••

The family identified a problem, looked for the underlying causes that reinforced the problem, and considered a solution—all in the context of a healing environment. Though the daughter may not have made the parents' choice easy—she could protest, throw a tantrum, or cry when they took her to school the next day—they had identified deeper concerns that contributed to their current dilemma.

Human nature tempts us to look for what seems to be the easy way out and refuses to look deeper into the reasons we act and feel as we do. As family leaders, parents need to continue to diagnose family needs and bring healing results.

I can recall the frustration I felt as a child when one of my elementary schoolteachers persistently told the class, "The answer is inside you. I'll teach you how to find it, but you're responsible for solving the problem." I was frustrated because I wanted her to give me the answer so that I wouldn't have to expend energy looking at all the possible solutions. In her wisdom, this teacher pushed me to look at all angles of a problem, knowing that in time my understanding would be complete.

I recognized this teacher's wisdom years later when I found myself helping my own children with life's daily dilemmas, be it homework or personal matters. My kids want me simply to tell them the answer. I often refuse, saying something similar to what my teacher told me years ago.

In family relationships, the same principle applies. Ginny's mother would have liked for someone else to deal with the dilemma of whether or not to force school attendance on her daughter. The husband initially wanted to force his own solution to the problem. But because these family leaders were willing to look beyond their own emotions, they arrived at a decision to their problem *and* discovered something about what the family needed for future growth.

Summary: As we try to look beyond our family members' behavior to the message behind the behavior, we must offer them our understanding, respect, and trustworthiness. To understand our family members, we must learn to look at the situation from the other person's point of view.

Only when we begin to understand the emotions beneath the behavior can we grow as a family. The next chapter will explore the role of emotions in family communications and will discuss whether emotions are good or bad.

1. Without being too analytical, take time in the next few days to observe the behavior of the different members of your family. Focus on the adults in your family as well as the children. As you try to understand them, ask these questions:

- What emotions did they show when they acted as they did?
- Is there a pattern to the way they behave? If so, what message does that pattern communicate?
- Am I reacting or responding to the behavior? Does my response cause the behavior to intensify or occur more frequently?
- How do they communicate this same message to others? Do they feel that anyone understands them? Do they seem to feel forced to show their feelings through exaggerated behavior?

2. After you have thought through these questions, be bold enough to ask your family members if your hunches are correct. If you have a child who is too young to discuss these matters, talk them over with your spouse or an adult friend. Note the difference in your reaction when your focus goes beyond the outward behavior. Use this exercise to help identify skills you can develop as you try to be more responsive to family needs.

3. Observe your behavior during the week. Ask yourself these questions:

- How do I communicate that I understand my family members?
- How do I show that I respect them?
- How do I assure them that they can trust me?

4. Identify one family member with whom you are having some conflict. How can you use understanding to diagnose the problem? How can you use understanding to develop a solution to the problem?

5. What two things will you do this week to show understanding to the family member with whom you feel in conflict?

6. In the famous love chapter (1 Corinthians 13), the apostle Paul details the qualities of a loving person. Where the qualities of love abound, understanding is hatched. Note the traits of love that Paul enumerates. Love is long-suffering, kind, and humble. Paul also names the action of love. Love behaves politely, considers others' needs, holds its temper, thinks healthy thoughts, delights in the truth, and is constant. We don't often think of love as a behavior that can be practiced and developed. We generally think of it as a feeling we express whenever we feel a surge of sentiment. Yet conveying love can become a habit when we develop good habits like those Paul lists in this passage. In what three ways will you demonstrate love to your family members this week?

CHAPTER THREE

What Are You Really Trying to Tell Me?

"**W**HY do I feel like this?"

"I don't know. Exactly how do you feel?"

Cathy was a thirty-something wife and mother of two school-age children. She was in her second marriage; her first husband abandoned her shortly after her second child was born. Though Cathy is still young, she looked at least ten years older than her age. She was obviously stressed and tired. Nonetheless, she was a pleasant woman who desperately wanted to gain a new direction in her life. The pleading tone in her voice begged for an answer to her question.

"It's hard to explain exactly how I feel. I feel lots of emotions all at the same time. I feel depressed. I feel worried. I feel determined. But probably more than anything, I feel guilty."

"Oh? How's that?"

"I feel as if I've sinned. I mean, why else would I feel

these things if something wasn't wrong with me? I feel as if my emotions are telling me I've royally messed up my life."

"Sinned?"

"Yeah. I mean, isn't it a sin to feel depressed? Why would I feel guilty if something in my life wasn't wrong?"

"Then your emotions are convicting you."

"They're convicting me that I've done something wrong."

"Then that's good."

"What? How can it be good to feel all these things I feel?"

"You mentioned that you feel determined. That was the only positive emotion you listed."

"I guess you could call it positive. What else can I be other than determined to make things better? I've still got many years ahead of me. I want to give my children a better life than I've had. And I want to make my marriage work. I don't want to go through the hell I went through in my first marriage."

"Then I would say it's good that you have those other emotions."

"Which ones? The depression? Guilt? Worry? Are you saying I should be glad to feel all those things?"

"Not exactly. I'm simply suggesting that each of those emotions has put you on guard against the bad things life has thrown at you. If you didn't feel anything at all, I would be worried about you. But since you feel these so-called negative emotions, I honestly believe that the chances are good that you'll change things for the better."

ARE EMOTIONS GOOD OR BAD?

Successful family life involves understanding not only other family members but also ourselves. Most of us are like Cathy: We want to understand what we feel and why we feel that way. I know that I feel charged with excitement when I uncover some unique thing that sets me apart as a person. My wife, Julie, and our three daughters also benefit when I learn more about what makes me tick. I would hope that each small bit of understanding I gain makes me easier to live with.

In our attempt to understand ourselves and others, however, we bump up against our emotions, many of which are confusing to us. Most of us use the following logic as we think about our feelings:

- I realize I am not perfect. I err (sin) every day.
- When I make mistakes (sin), I have an emotional reaction.
- Often, my emotions create more problems (more sin) than they erase.
- Therefore, some emotions are bad (sinful) emotions. I need to avoid them.

When we sin, we suffer consequences. Sin produces alienation from both God and other people. Sin keeps us from being all we are meant to be. Ultimately, sin causes death, both spiritual and physical. But ignoring our emotions does not correct the effects of sin. In fact, it weakens our attempt to correct what we know to be wrong in our lives.

It makes perfectly good logic, doesn't it, to categorize our feelings as good or bad? Somehow, we feel better when we can pigeonhole our feelings into neat bundles.

Doing so tells us which emotions to shun and which ones to perfect. We tend to push several emotions to the top of the "negative emotions" list: anger, jealousy, guilt, pride, and worry.

For families to move forward, we need to understand the vital role human emotions play in shaping our family relationships. I like to steer people away from the notion that an emotion *must* be negative simply because it is associated with conflict. We need to live with the paradox that *emotions can hurt a person if they are expressed and they can hurt a person if they are withheld.* Certainly, the misuse of an emotion may lead to negative consequences, but at its core an emotion is not necessarily bad. God gave us all emotions with a specific design. Understanding the purpose of our feelings helps us discover their potential value. If family members understand the reason for an emotional reaction—whether that emotion seems good or bad—they can learn to deal more effectively with the conflict that often surrounds it.

THE CONNECTION BETWEEN EMOTIONS AND FAMILY COMMUNICATION

Allow me to suggest a new logic as we contemplate the feelings and actions that pervade family life.

- Each person is a creation of God, made with the potential to become a positive force within the family.
- No one is perfect. All persons are going to make mistakes, including the mistake of misusing the emotions that are a part of God's design.

- Every family member can learn to become sensitive to the message attached to every emotion.
- All emotions are God given and have a positive use. They become negative when we misuse them or use them in an imbalanced way.
- As family members begin to understand the purpose of various emotions, they are more likely to become the positive people God intends them to be.

This understanding of human emotions allows a complete cycle to take shape. It recognizes the reality of sin, but it provides for the healing that accompanies grace and forgiveness. One role of the family leader is to help family members move from unfulfilled potential toward a complete and fully functioning unit. At the root of this growth cycle is the need to recognize and understand the basic value of individual emotions.

Let's look at two vignettes of family situations in which emotions are out of balance, signaling a need for an in-depth evaluation of the meaning of those feelings.

Situation: Kendra was angry with her husband for coming home late from the golf course. When he walked through the back door in the middle of the afternoon, she greeted him with a blast. "What do you think you're doing, playing golf all day long? You said you would be home a little after noon, and here it is almost three o'clock. There's still plenty that needs to be done around here, and the day is almost shot! When are you going to mow the grass? You promised me this morning that you would have it done before my parents come tonight. How do you expect to get the yard cleaned up and then get showered and shaved before six o'clock? I'll bet you didn't think about that while you were out having a good time with your buddies, did you?"

"Wait just a minute! For your information, I came home earlier than I could have. I tried to call you to let you know I was going to get something to eat with Fred and Dale, but every time I called, the line was busy. I've still got plenty of time to do everything I need to do before your parents come over. Luke is going to help me. I told him I would give him extra allowance if he did."

"I wish you wouldn't do this to me. How do I know if you're going to do all you say you will? I don't want this place looking like a dump when we have company coming over! Just promise me it won't happen again!"

"Honey, I tried to touch base with you several times today but couldn't reach you on the phone. I'm sorry if I upset you. I'll get the yard work done. Don't worry about that."

Analysis: Kendra had a legitimate concern: She wanted the yard to look nice before her parents came to their house for dinner. Nothing wrong with that. She became upset when it appeared that her husband might not get home in time to mow the grass as he had promised. She was merely showing her concern when she exploded as he walked in the back door. Her desire to avoid an undesirable situation was darkened by her angry outburst. Being offensive toward her husband overshadowed her intent to make a potentially wrong situation right. The emotion of anger was not necessarily wrong, but its aggressive expression was damaging, making its effect negative.

• • • •

Situation: "Mom! Would you come in here?" The
urgency in Belinda's voice served as a signal that something bad was about to happen.

"What's the problem, Belinda?" asked her mom, who
tried to sound calm as she stood in the doorway of the
bedroom Belinda shared with her younger sister.

"It's that bratty little Heather. I'm trying to find my
library book, and she won't even help me. Can you tell
her to get up and look for my book or else get out of here?"

Belinda's mom noticed that Heather was crying.
Instead of responding immediately to Belinda, the
mother asked Heather, "What's the problem?"

"Belinda pinched me because I wouldn't help her
find her stupid book," wailed Heather.

Belinda quickly defended herself. "I had to, Mom! I
couldn't get her to cooperate with me!" With those
words, Belinda joined her sister in crying. It was all their
mom could do to keep from breaking out with tears of
her own.

Analysis: The primary emotion Belinda showed was impatience. Several other emotions spun off from that
central feeling, including irritability, intolerance, self-
centeredness, and disgust. She wanted relief from a situation that made her feel uncomfortable. She had misplaced a library book and wanted to find it so she could
return it. No parent could disagree with that notion. The
child's impatience was fueled, though, by her own stubborn self-absorption. Belinda's overstatement of a valid
request encouraged her mother to focus on repairing the
damage the girl had done to her younger sister.

THE FUNCTION OF KEY EMOTIONS

Belinda and Heather's mom focused on the emotional outburst and not on the content of messages underlying her daughters' behavior. She—and we—need to learn to look beyond overworked feelings to the hidden but valid emotional expression.

Understanding key emotions can help families move away from emotional entanglement and frustration toward harmony and growth. Earlier in this chapter we identified several emotions that at first glance seem to be negative emotions: anger, jealousy, guilt, pride, and worry. Let's take a closer look at these emotions, discovering ways they can influence us both positively and negatively.

Anger. On the positive side, anger can motivate us to stand up for what we believe is right. It can help us correct a situation that is out of balance and advocate for the truth. On the negative side, overworked anger may signal insensitivity. It may be fueled by a desire to feel superior to others, which in turn suggests weak self-esteem.

Jealousy. On the positive side, jealousy signals a need for affirmation. The underlying message of the jealous person is, "Do you think I am a worthwhile person? I hope you do." It is normal and positive for each of us to want to be told that we "belong" to someone. Jealousy asks for that basic need to be met. On the negative side, excessive jealousy fears that love will be lost, or at least diminished, and pushes us toward hostility. The behaviors that accompany jealousy often cause the very reactions we do not want: arguments, withheld affection, resentment, and lack of respect. Others feel smothered by this emotion and will often run from it.

Guilt. On the positive side, guilt helps us feel remorse for something we have done wrong. Confessing a wrongdoing may lead us to experience forgiveness from others. Guilt is often a prime motivator of change. When we feel a healthy sense of guilt, we will work to rebuild past failures. On the negative side, overworked guilt can cause us to be unnecessarily hard on ourselves. Failing to understand the freedom of forgiveness, we may isolate ourselves and begin to feel hopeless and depressed.

Pride. On the positive side, pride suggests a positive feeling about our personal accomplishments. It reflects a healthy self-concept. Pride may motivate us to excel. On the negative side, imbalanced pride may make us selfish, encouraging us to look out for our personal needs at the expense of others' needs. We may end up with an exaggerated sense of our importance and a harshly critical attitude toward others. The result can be failure both in relationships and in personal achievement.

Worry. On the positive side, worry frequently results from genuine concern for ourselves or others. We think of the long-term harm that might result if a negative situation goes unchecked. The tension that accompanies worry may spur us to action and can serve as protection against harm. On the negative side, overworked worry can result in irrational thinking or paranoia. The people about whom we are worrying may feel smothered by unwanted protection. Worry can take its toll on the body, causing a variety of physical reactions.

These are but a few of the emotions that can dominate family life. Understanding common feelings allows family members to recognize how the emotional climate of the home can either help or hinder family relations. They need not view the emotions that dominate family life as positive or negative. Instead, they should see them as either useful or harmful in building the family's communication network. Family members should learn to perceive more accurately their emotions and their potential effect on relationships.

BRING EMOTIONS INTO BALANCE

When we feel uncomfortable with a family member's emotion, we may tell that person, "Don't feel that way." In doing that, we suggest that certain emotions are bad or unacceptable. Perhaps a more effective message would be, "Bring your emotions into balance." Jesus taught us that sin is more than a violation of rules. Sin is whatever causes relationships to go sour. In the great Sermon on the Mount, he taught that what is in the heart (our emotions) is more important than our actions (Matthew 5:20-48).

Read the following family scenarios depicting emotions that are out of balance. Note that the emotion itself is not necessarily wrong, but the warped expression of it can be harmful.

Situation: For most of their childhood, Dennis and Hal had been best friends. After years of being neighbors, Hal and his family moved to a different house, but he and Dennis still saw each other daily at school. Hal made friends in his new neighborhood and soon began to ignore Dennis in favor of his other buddies. Dennis understandably felt rejected. Seeking solace, he talked with his mother.

"Mom, Hal acts as if he doesn't even know me anymore. It's as if he forgot that we've grown up together. I hate him for the way he's treating me."

Concerned at her son's choice of words, Mom replied, "Maybe you don't like what Hal is doing, but that doesn't mean you hate him."

"Yes, it does! How would you like it if you sat down by him and said hello and he didn't even answer? He acts as if I'm not even there. That's totally rude, Mom, and I hate him for it!"

Realizing she would get nowhere by telling her son not to hate Hal, his mother shifted her focus. "Well, what do you plan to do about it?"

"I've already done something about," came the indignant reply.

The mom asked hesitantly, "Exactly what did you do?"

With a hard look on his face, Dennis coldly said, "I told him in front of his new friends that he was being rude and that he was no longer my friend. And then I told the other guys sitting there that they had better watch out because Hal's the kind who will leave you as soon as he finds someone better. Then he said some stuff back to me, and we got into it."

"A fight?"

"Yes, Mom. A fight! And I don't care one bit what Hal thinks of me now because we're not friends anymore."

Analysis: Dennis had a strong emotion that he labeled "hate." His mother was right in thinking that hate is an ugly emotion, for it is. Reducing Dennis's emotion to its smaller parts, we can see that hatred is actually a stockpile of other emotions. Beneath hatred are also anger, fear, worry, and rejection. Examined separately, each of them is valid. It is understandable that Dennis would feel angry and rejected at being excluded by his best friend. And it's logical for him to be afraid and worry that he could not replace what had been a meaningful relationship.

Dennis's emotions became a liability not because they were invalid emotions but because they had become imbalanced. His skewed feelings led him to act irresponsibly. He started a fight that not only could have done physical damage but also could have further fractured a friendship.

Dennis's mom could help him bring his emotions back into balance by acknowledging their existence. She could say to him, "You *hate* Hal? That's a strong word." In doing so, she acknowledges his feelings and shows a willingness to let Dennis say what he feels— even if it is harsh. As parents we fear that acknowledging a child's tough emotions only fertilizes them and causes them to grow stronger. Yet the opposite is true. Talking about feelings helps kids deal with them, preventing them from being overstated.

••••

Situation: Jack had a bad habit of criticizing his family. He was a perfectionist who liked to see things done the right way. In Jack's mind, the right way was synonymous with *his* way. He was forever reminding his wife to take care of trivial duties that could have easily waited until later. When he talked with the children, he chewed on them for what they had done wrong rather than praise them for what they had done right. If one of the kids made a 99 on a test at school, Jack's first question was, "So what did you miss on the test?"

Kimberly's stomach stayed tied in knots over her husband's perfectionistic ways. She knew it would do no good to reason with Jack. She had tried that before and had fallen prey to Jack's powerful persuasion. He masterfully rationalized everything he did. Instead, she worked on her children, telling them things such as, "Just ignore him when he talks to you like that" or "He doesn't know what he's talking about. He thinks he's right, but he's not" or "We don't have to let Daddy know everything. What he doesn't know won't hurt him, and it might save all of us a lecture."

Jack and Kimberly's children learned that they could split their parents by getting them to argue. Kimberly's plan to soothe her children's suffering self-esteem back-fired as she witnessed the kids become increasingly confused about how to respect either parent.

Analysis: Kimberly held her husband in contempt for his overbearing ways. She was justified in her emotional pain because his ways were rigid and annoying. Her sensitivity became tainted, however, as her emotions were smothered with bitterness. When her feelings persuaded her to encourage her children to disdain their father's ways, she contributed to further family breakdown.

Kimberly was right in feeling that her children needed a buffer against their father's controlling ways. But the imbalance of her own emotions caused her to want her children to side with her. Their actual need was to feel understood in light of the harsh demands that had been laid on them. In the end, her influence over her children diminished.

Kimberly could become an effective family leader if

she would let her children draw their own conclusions about their father. By trying to push her beliefs on her kids, she left them without an adult with whom they could talk openly about their confusion. The likelihood that Kimberly's children would retreat to their own private world of thoughts was strong. She can help bring Jack's emotions into balance by controlling her own bitterness. Though she need not give in to Jack's controlling ways, fighting his rigidity is sure to cause further marital strife. Her influence with both Jack and their children will rise as she effectively manages her own feelings.

WHAT DO OUR EMOTIONS TELL US?

As I study how families function, I am constantly reminded that my family is just like any other. My wife, daughters, and I experience a full range of emotions. We come at family life with our own perceptions and experiences. We are all at varied stages of life's cycle. We have differing understandings of our family's inter-actions. We ask each other, Why did you do that? And just like any other family, we experience discomfort. It helps me to recall simple exchanges among my family members as I try to understand how to help others understand their own family dynamics.

My memory draws me to one of those nights when our family had little to do. I do not recall, but surely it was a dark and stormy night since the entire family was cloaked in a dour mood. The atmosphere was ripe, I suppose, for complaining. I believe I was the one who started the ball rolling.

Peering at the roll around my stomach, I said to no

one in particular, "I need to start working out harder. This paunch is getting bigger by the minute."

Julie knew just the right response. "Looking at your gut and talking about it won't get rid of it. The gym is open every day of the week, you know." Those blunt words did little to soothe my woeful frame of mind.

Moments later Emily, our older teenager, took the cue from me and muttered, "I'm not doing so hot in my geometry class. I might make a C. That would be the first C I've had on a report card. I wish my grade was higher."

Her younger sister Sarah had no sympathy for her dilemma. "So why aren't you upstairs studying?"

"Because it's Friday. What do you expect?"

"I expect you're going to make a C on your report card."

Even Mary, our youngest, got into the act. "I can't find the book I'm supposed to be reading. It's in my room somewhere, but I don't know where."

Once again Julie had the perfect solution. "If your room were cleaned up, you would have no problem finding things. Did you ever think of that?"

Mary, having learned from her older sisters how to put off a pushy parent, rolled her eyes and moaned, "Oh, Mom!"

Emily, Mary, and I had one thing in common that night: We were uncomfortable about something. I was dissatisfied with a few unwanted pounds around the waist. Emily was upset at a potentially low geometry grade. Mary was frustrated over a cluttered bedroom. The answer given to each of us was exactly the same. Sure the words were varied, but the message was: *If you are uncomfortable about your plight in life, do something about it. Change things!*

Christians have long struggled with the matter of discomfort. We give names to the sources of discomfort: sin, evil, disobedience, wrongdoing. Try as we may, we cannot outrun it. Difficult circumstances pop up wherever we turn. Just when it seems that we have succeeded in straightening out all of life's crumpled edges, new adversities visit us. Or worse yet, old troubles return to haunt us.

God has no intention of deliberately making life hard on families. In fact, I firmly believe he means for us to have the opposite. He wants family life to be pleasurable. A well-known verse tells us, "And we know that in all things God works for the good of those who love him, who have been called according to his purpose" (Romans 8:28). While life does not promise us a joyride, we are assured that the dregs of life are not a permanent feature. Families can fight back at life's misfortunes.

The following case study demonstrates how discomfort in a family can lead to positive growth.

CASE STUDY: KENT'S DOWNFALL TURNS HIS FAMILY AROUND

Mrs. Cauthon casually answered the ringing telephone, not expecting the incoming message from the other end of the line.

"Mrs. Cauthon, this is Mrs. Gerik calling from Kent's school."

Immediately, Mrs. Cauthon knew that her fifteen-year-old son was in trouble. The tone in the school counselor's voice was grim, not cheery as it would be if she were calling with good news. The mom swallowed and sat down on the stool next to the phone.

"Yes? How are you, Mrs. Gerik? I hope things are going well."

Getting to the point of her message, Mrs. Gerik explained, "Things could be better. I hate to tell you this, but Kent was absent from school today. He was also out Monday afternoon. He gave us an excuse for his absences, but I'm suspicious and thought I had better give you a call to verify a few things."

Wanting to cooperate fully with the counselor, Mrs. Cauthon said with a decided sound in her voice, "I can tell you that Kent has not been sick. He hasn't had any appointments that would take him away from school either. What do you need from me? I'll help in any way you suggest."

Grateful for Mrs. Cauthon's cooperative spirit, Mrs. Gerik suggested, "Let the school handle the discipline. We'll take care of that. You can help us by emphasizing to Kent that you want to take a bad situation and use it to help him turn his attitude around. I don't want Kent so threatened that he rebels against all of us, but I think he should realize that he has responsibilities to uphold."

Over the course of the next few days, Kent's parents had several talks with him. Before confronting their son, the parents resolved not to allow their discussions with him to degenerate into verbal free-for-alls. They had been that route before and were disinterested in fighting with their son any more than was absolutely necessary.

Making a point to listen to Kent's complaints and excuses, no matter how distasteful, they gained several valuable insights into his view of the family. First, Kent believed that no other person in the family took the time to see life as he did. From his view, the other family members were so self-absorbed that they ignored one another. He felt estranged from his own family. Second, he shared that he was bothered more than his parents realized by their marital spats. Rather than dismiss their frequent verbal skirmishes as an adult matter that should be ignored, he took their brawls personally, believing that something was seriously wrong in their home. Third, he revealed that his behavior marked his way of communicating his personal heartache. More than he could verbalize, he was grieved by the sour state of his family's affairs. Through his behavior he was screaming, "I feel helpless to change things around here! Does anyone share my suffering?"

The Cauthons' past tendency had been to react by counterattacking their son's accusations. They would have sent their own messages to him. These may have included the following:

- "It's your own fault that you feel separated from the rest of the family. How can we include you when you refuse to communicate with us? You spend so much time locked up in your room that we've simply assumed that you don't want us to include you."
- "What we say and do to each other is our business and no one else's, especially not yours. Besides, half of our squabbles are about you. If you would straighten up, maybe we wouldn't have so many fights."
- "If you've got something to say to us, then say it! How are we supposed to know what you mean

when you act out your feelings? Are you playing
charades with us? Do you think we can read your
mind?"

However, instead of reacting to Kent, the Cauthons
tried to understand their son's point of view. They
maintained their position of family leadership by avoiding needless arguments with their son, and they made
the following four adjustments:

First, following the counselor's suggestion to allow
the school to discipline Kent for his misconduct, they
did not pronounce a penalty against him. They
assumed that the teenager would realize that they disagreed with his poor judgment. They quietly stood
behind the school's decision.

Second, the parents made a greater effort to supervise
Kent's activities. They made a point to be better
informed of his whereabouts. They talked more frequently with his friends' parents, ensuring proper supervision when necessary. They kept in close contact with
Mrs. Gerik so that school problems could be dealt with
before they got out of hand.

Third, the family emphasized activities they could do
together. The Cauthons made family relationships a
priority, whether that was sitting on the edge of their
son's bed as he readied himself for sleep, playing board
games with him after supper, or dining out as a family.

Fourth, heeding their son's concern about their relationship, Mr. and Mrs. Cauthon enriched their marriage by
spending more time with one another. Even though Kent
was not always a witness to their activities, they talked
with each other, helped each other out with daily chores,

and went on periodic dates. Their improved rapport with one another spilled over into family life.

••••

In the end, the discomfort that Kent's negative behavior brought to the family led them to a place of growth. We often pray to God to take an uncomfortable situation and bring good from it. If God would answer us aloud, I believe he might say, "There is nothing more that I want for you than the best life has to offer." But he would also likely add, "You are the channel I must use to change things. You must decide to improve those things you can. I will be the source of your strength."

Kent's choice of behavior was poor. Yet in some ways it signaled his discomfort with his family relationships. His parents were uncomfortable with his conduct too. It was this discomfort that provided the catalyst for improvements in their home. Notice how the solution to their family problem was multifaceted:

- The school administered punishment to Kent. The parents were supportive of the school's efforts and followed up by tightening their own supervision.
- Kent's parents never denied him the right to feel the way he felt. Though they privately disagreed with him, they recognized that it was Kent's job, not theirs, to make sense of his uncomfortable emotions.
- The parents made a conscious effort to remember that Kent was a teenager who viewed responsibilities differently from how adults viewed them. Although they refused to compromise their own

personal convictions, they did not try to force
him to think as they did. He was a teenager and
was at a different stage in life than they were.
• When Kent expressed irritation or discomfort
about the discipline the school administered, his
parents recognized his discomfort as positive.
They made no attempt to take away that uncomfortable feeling. And they did not say or do
things that would make him feel worse. They
allowed time to be its own healing agent.

God sends answers to prayers in ways we do not
always recognize. By opening ourselves to healthy ways
of tackling family concerns, we become the route
through which God communicates to our children. Our
openness to the veiled messages sent by family members makes God's will in our family life more evident.

WHEN DISCOMFORT BECOMES OVERWHELMING
Discomfort can be a motivator. There is little doubt
about that fact. Yet sometimes the discomfort can
become so overwhelming that despair sets in, refusing
to loosen its grip on the family. Consider the following
comments by family members:

Indignant child: If they think I won't fight back,
just watch me! They'll really be sorry for what they
did when I run away!

Abused wife: The only thing that keeps me from
swallowing a bottle of pills is my children. I wish I
were dead.

Bitter husband: I'm in charge of this house. I aim to do things the way they're supposed to be done. And if everyone else gets upset with me, then so be it!

Defeated teenager: I honestly wonder if anyone knows I exist. My own family doesn't seem to care about me.

••••

Family problems like these cannot be fixed easily. To be sure, the family can make adjustments that will alleviate the pain of the emotionally wounded family member. But beyond the physical adjustments the family leaders might make is a need for change in family communication. The most basic communication tool available to uncomfortable families is the skill of listening and expressing understanding. Feeling understood allows the disheartened member to profit from other adjustments. Consider the reaction of the hurt family member when listening occurs.

To the indignant child: You want to be taken seriously. Even though you're just eight years old, your feelings are important to you. Sometimes it seems that we ignore you.

To the abused wife: Life hasn't been fair. Sometimes it seems so bad, you wish it were over.

To the bitter husband: Nothing's going the way you think it should go. It's enough to make you blow your stack.

> **To the defeated teenager:** We've all been so busy, we haven't given you the attention you deserve. It's little wonder you feel deserted.

••••

Perhaps consoling words do not come easily to some family members. A husband or father not accustomed to affirming his wife or children may find that words become stuck in his throat when he attempts an understanding comment. Or a weary woman may retreat from her children in silence following yet another rough verbal exchange. Even though skill is required in showing understanding to others, like any other skill, it can be learned.

As family members learn to give listening responses, they will move toward growth, even if progress is slow. A gruff father can touch his son in a way that says, "Even though I can't put my feelings into words, I'm trying to see things the way you do." A wounded mother might have to bite her tongue so that she can approach her daughter in love once her emotions have settled. A proud husband may need to practice saying "I'm sorry" before he moves toward deeper communication.

When discomfort is so burdensome that it becomes a barrier to emotional growth, family members must do what they can to ease the heavy weight of that discomfort so that real change can follow. I am convinced that just as God does not desire, and certainly does not cause, discomfort to settle on his children, parents do not intentionally bring harm on families. And as God relies on each of us to be agents of change in his world, we can also start the change process in our families.

The writer of Proverbs gives wise instruction when he writes, "A gentle answer turns away wrath" (Proverbs 15:1). Once anger, hurt, fear, discouragement, and all the other feelings that accompany discomfort are lessened, change can begin. The probability that families will move forward increases.

Summary: All emotions are valid. However, when they are out of balance, they can cause family conflict. Sometimes the discomfort created by a strong expression of emotions can lead to positive change. Family leaders can help the family grow by listening and responding to the emotional messages behind the behavior.

The last three chapters have explored skills that will move family leaders away from reacting to behavior and toward responding to the underlying message. We have learned to observe and interpret family behavior as we seek to understand how our families function.

Part 2 will focus on understanding how five family behavior patterns—rigidity, dependence, argumentativeness, withdrawal, and indulgence—influence family communication and conflict.

FAMILY NOTES

1. One of the most effective ways family members can help one another understand their emotions is to encourage verbal communication of those feelings. Listening is an important family communication tool. When family members feel understood, they feel better not only about themselves but also about the other person. To show that you are actively listening, use phrases like the following:

- "It seems to you . . ."
- "You mean . . . ?"
- "I get the impression that . . ."
- "It's hard for you to . . ."
- "What makes sense to you is . . ."
- "Tell me if this is what you feel . . ."
- "Is it possible that you feel . . . ?"
- "Somewhere deep inside you . . ."
- "Others don't feel this way, but you . . ."
- "The way you figure it . . ."
- "It's hard for you not to feel . . ."
- "Do you mean . . . ?"
- "Even though you didn't say it, you're . . ."
- "From your experience it seems . . ."

2. Consider the following scenarios. Put yourself in the place of each of these family members. Ask yourself what the person might be feeling. Try to perceive the potential emotions that could be swelling inside the individual.

Take into account age and developmental factors as you try to see the world from the person's position.

> **Mother of young children:** I stay mad at my kids all the time. If I have something important to do, that's when they decide to romp through the house. They run in and out of the room I'm in, asking a million questions and placing all these demands on me. I try to explain that I'm busy, and they ignore me.
>
> **Mother's feelings:** _____
>
> _____
>
> **Teenage boy:** Tell me what you think about this! I was late to class the other day. My teacher got mad at me the way she always does. I told her she needed to calm down. She got her face right in mine and started yelling at me. I got mad and cussed at her. She deserved it too! She sent me to the office. I was suspended from school for three days, and she didn't get anything!
>
> **Teenager's feelings:** _____
>
> _____
>
> **Middle-aged man:** My wife accuses me of ignoring my family duties. She says I spend too much time at the office. She wants us to do more together as a family, but everything she suggests costs money. She doesn't understand. I'm not ignoring the family; I'm just trying to stay ahead of all our bills.

Man's feelings: _____

_____

3. Having practiced with these examples, choose one of your own family members. Identify a behavior or a recent situation you are trying to understand. Try to look at that situation in a new light. What behavior did your family member display? What emotion was the person trying to express? How can you respond to the emotion without reacting to the behavior? How will you do that in the next two days?

4. Spend some time in the next few days closely examining yourself. Try to be as honest with yourself as you can. Look at yourself the way the rest of your family does. Become aware of how your spouse and children view you. While it is not necessary that you try to conform to all expectations others have of you, take into account the feedback you are given. The Bible is filled with words that encourage personal introspection and growth. Read each of the following verses or passages as a guide to spiritual improvement:

- Psalm 139:23-24
- Proverbs 1:20–2:22
- Matthew 5:3-10
- Mark 10:43-45
- 1 Corinthians 13:1-13
- Galatians 6:1-5
- Ephesians 6:10-17
- Philippians 2:5-16

5. As important as it is to focus on your other family members, don't neglect your own emotional needs. Seek personal balance. Avoid the two extremes of hiding your emotions and expressing them with no restraint.

Understand Your Family's Patterns

Rigidity: Refusing to Budge

FRIDAY afternoon finally arrived. Friday afternoon—the best time of the week for a ten-year-old boy. Baker Slade did what he did most afternoons after school. He quickly devoured a doughnut left over from the morning's breakfast and zipped outside to ride his bike. Even the air that sped past his face told him he was free to do as he pleased. It was time to relax.

Baker liked to pretend that his bicycle was a Harley-Davidson. At his command, the vehicle could do whatever he demanded. It could barrel down the street as fast as greased lightning, or it could cruise smoothly and slowly so others could stop and admire it. When Baker was on his bike, he felt as if he was king of the world, or at least of his part of it.

The spirited youth found his best friend, Zach, and they rode through the streets and alleys in their neighborhood. Occasionally the friends stopped to get off their bikes. Once, they timed each other to see who could climb to the third branch of Mrs. Darcus's red oak tree first. Another time, they paused to peer inside a trash bin because Baker thought he saw a rat run inside it. Otherwise, the boys spent a carefree hour roaming their domain on their bikes.

At 5:30 Zach told Baker he had to go home. His mother had told him they would be going out that evening. Though Baker was not yet ready to put his bike away for the night, he concluded that he should check in with his mother too. Dad would be home soon, and Baker did not want to be missing when Dad got home. One thing about Baker's dad was that once he arrived home, he wanted to know where everyone was and what the plans were for the rest of the evening. He did not like surprises.

Thoughtlessly, Baker did just as he always did when he wheeled into the driveway leading to the back of the house. He skidded to a screeching halt, dropped his bike to the concrete below him, and strolled into the house. Informing his mother that he was home, Baker found a parking space in front of the television and flipped on the set, planning to stay put until someone told him it was time to do something else.

Moments later, Baker heard his dad's car pull into the drive. As a troubling thought forced its way to the front of his mind, he mumbled to himself, "Uh-oh." Sure enough, he heard the car door slam once, then again, and finally a third time. Pretending to be innocent of any wrongdoing, Baker stared at the television as his father walked into the house and immediately found his son.

Without as much as a simple hello, Dad growled, "Who left a bike in the driveway *again?*"

Baker wanted to taunt his father and ask if perhaps that bike in the driveway was his mom's. Or maybe he could sarcastically claim that fourteen-month-old Bethany had learned to ride a bicycle and must have left it where it should not be.

Instead, he simply mumbled, "Sorry."

"Sorry! Is that all you can say? Sorry! Baker, how many times have I told you to put away your bike when you're through riding it? Huh? Probably at least five hundred times, wouldn't you say? When are you ever going to learn that you're supposed to put your things away when you're not using them?"

"I was going to ride it again after supper."

"I don't care when you were going to ride it again. If you're not sitting on top of that bike, I want it out of the driveway! Understood?"

"Yes, sir."

Dad stomped out of the room as Baker crawled off the couch to follow his father's request, if that was what his ultimatum could be called. The familiar knot formed in his stomach. Though Baker didn't dare voice his feelings, he mused to himself, "Why should I do what Dad asks me to do? When did he ever tell me thanks?"

••••

Baker's family endured constant conflict, most of it in the evening, when his dad was home. Baker noticed that whenever his dad was around, his mom's personality changed. She became silent, timid, and afraid, trying to avoid her husband's angry outbursts. The whole family had become victims of Jim Slade's rigidity.

Jim was unaware of the impact of his behavior on his family. In fact, he thought of himself as a successful husband and father. When he spoke, his son obeyed. What could be better? His way of solving family problems was simple. State a rule, and then expect it to be followed. No questions allowed.

Though Baker's dad quickly fixed the problem of minor irresponsibility, he ignored more important family problems and emotional needs. He was blind to Baker's need for affirmation and encouragement. He failed to see that Baker felt ignored, even insignificant. Jim Slade was oblivious to his wife's fear and sadness. As long as she did what he expected, he was happy with her. And he assumed she was happy too.

RIGIDITY

Rigidity often expresses itself in rules, punishments, and prescriptions for change. But it also wears other guises:

• Luke has just experienced his first failing grade on a report card. He struggles with a learning disability but had always managed to pass his classes, even though school was a laborious effort. He tried to explain his frustration to his parents, but they would not listen. Instead, they gave him a lengthy lecture and told him they expected better things of him.

• Even though sixteen-year-old Shannon knew her family was strapped for money, she demanded a car shortly after her birthday. She reminded her parents that they had assured her she would have a vehicle when she was old enough to drive. Her parents reasoned with her, explaining that their financial situation had taken a turn for the worse in the last year. Unwilling to listen to her parents, the girl simply said, "But you promised!"

• A single mother found herself in an endless battle with her former husband. He refused to budge when she wanted to change their visitation schedule with the children. Convinced that the only way to get through to him was to "fight fire with fire," she requested a court hearing with the intent of having her former husband increase his child-support payments to her. "It will serve him right," she vindictively thought.

Rigidity, whatever form it takes, wears on family relationships. Whether parents will not relax their standards, a child makes insistent demands, or adults are unyielding, the net result is a breakdown in relationships. The following are signs of emotional rigidity within the home:

- Rules are all-important.
- Approval comes only after compliance to rules.
- Achievements and accomplishments are more important than relationships.
- The letter of the law is more important than the spirit of the law.
- Strong emphasis is given to staying in charge or in control.
- Problem solving is based on logic rather than emotional considerations.
- The focus is on sin more than grace and forgiveness.
- Being right is more important than being understanding.

- Relationships tend to be stiff rather than warm.
- Physical affection is rarely demonsrated.

WHAT MESSAGE LIES BENEATH RIGIDITY?

Maybe you find yourself reacting to the pattern of rigidity in a family member. Maybe you are the rigid one, and your family members are reacting to you. Whatever the case, the question remains: What are rigid people really saying? What message lies beneath rigid behavior?

As much as rigid family members may want to loosen up and shake off their rigidity, fear often prevents them from action. Underneath their rigid, brusque behavior lies fear—*fear of losing control.* Listen to these rationalizations family members may offer as reasons for their rigid behavior:

- "If I let go of my standards for even one minute, this family will fall apart. I don't want to lose control of the home."
- "I've got so many emotions inside me, there's no telling what I might do if I let them come out."
- "I don't want to be manipulated by anyone. I've had that happen before, and I have vowed never to let anyone control me again."
- "You just can't trust people with your feelings. If you do, you'll get burned. Believe me, I know."
- "I'm really not very good at showing my feelings. I don't want to be laughed at for the way I express myself."

Can you sense the fear in these statements? It's odd how emotionally rigid people, who depict themselves as dauntless and unflinching, can be so dominated by apprehensions and anxiety. But as is so often the case with human emotions, exaggerated expressions of emotions often signal weak development of opposite emotions. We fear those emotions we know to be personal shortcomings.

Lest we be too hard on the rigid person, I want to point out that good intentions often motivate emotional stiffness. Recall that every emotion we experience has a potentially positive use. Looking beneath rigidity, we can see that its stiff exterior hides reasonable intentions, which include the intent to instill discipline, to breed success, to teach personal responsibility, to inspire respect for others, and to motivate others to achieve.

Rigid family members can offer excellent reasons for their behavior. In their mind, it makes sense to push hard for excellence. After all, the potential results are rewarding. Yet as with any trait that is imbalanced, rigidity can emphasize achievement to the exclusion of other important family needs, namely the need for emotional ties. A rigid person may say things like:

- "I only want what's best for the family. If I have to force the issue, I'm willing to do it, even if it means I'm the bad guy."
- "I want to make sure to get my point across. I believe very strongly in what I'm trying to say and want to make sure others understand."
- "In the past, I've felt ignored. I've learned that to be heard, I have to be forceful, and I can't budge an inch. I'm not trying to make people mad. I just want to be heard."

- "Nobody else around here has the courage to take a stand on tough family matters. I want this family to go places, even if I have to provoke everyone to action."

While these statements may sound positive, they mask the person's need to correct or control behavior. That need to control prevents the person from giving any thought to other people's emotional needs.

As I talk with rigid adults and children, several themes surface. Listen for the fearful themes of the following family members:

Preschool child: She took it from me first, and I want it back. It's mine and nobody else's. *(holds tightly to object while simultaneously striking an inflexible pose)*

Comment: Rigidity may rise from a desire to control others. Rigid behavior becomes tighter when people fear they will not be allowed to exercise their free will.

••••

Father: I'm sorry I have to yell at all of you to get you to turn out the lights and go to bed. But if that's what it takes to make you go to sleep, then so be it! You kids have no respect for authority. It's time you learned to do what you're told the first time I say it.

Comment: Rigidity may result from impatience. People who struggle with impatience may fear that their position of importance in the home is being challenged.

••••

Wife: You always make such a mess of this house. Anywhere you go, you leave a trail of trash, clothes, newspapers, or something! I feel as if I'm the only one around here who cares what this place looks like. Either you do your share of cleaning up around here or you can look for another wife. I refuse to be your maid!

Comment: Self-absorption can result in rigid expectations. Demanding that others conform to a single set of standards is a perfect setup for relationship failure, even though those standards may be valid.

••••

Teenager: You can accuse me of being irritable if you want to. When you tell me I have to do things I don't want to do, I'm going to refuse every time. I hate it when you push your way on me.

Comment: Rigidity is an emotional cousin to anger. When rigid reactions surface, anger is sure to appear.

UNLOCKING RIGIDITY'S HOLD ON THE FAMILY

As we understand the message behind the behavior of rigid people, we can often agree with their motivation, though we may disagree with their blueprint for action. A soft, tactful response often serves to calm rigidity, making it more likely that rigid behavior will give way to sensitivity. The antidote to rigidity is a response that says: Our family needs to recognize both behavior and feelings. Note how this wife's understanding calms her husband's rigidity.

> *Husband:* I'm sick of the way those kids push me to buy them whatever they want. They think I'm made of money. From now on, they have to earn what they get from me.

> *Wife:* Sometimes it seems that the kids don't appreciate what we give them, doesn't it?

> *Husband:* Sometimes! How about all the time? When I was their age, I would've loved to have everything they have. My dad was twice as strict as I am. It burns me to listen to them say I'm so hard on them. They don't know the meaning of hard times.

> *Wife:* There's probably a part of you that would like the kids to live as rough a life as you did when you were young, but then you've said before you wouldn't put them through what you endured even if you had to.

> *Husband:* No, I wouldn't. *(pauses and sighs)* I don't know, sometimes it seems that I just can't get through to them. I love them more than they know, but it hurts me to see them be so self-centered. Maybe it's my fault. Maybe I've spoiled them. That's why I'm so hard on them. I have to

make up for my own mistakes. Sometimes I feel like a failure as a father.

Wife: When you come down hard on the kids, you don't mean to drive them away. You want to teach them something. I know that, and you know that. I wouldn't call that being a bad father. You want what's best for them. But maybe there's another way to get through to them.

Husband: What do you think? You think I'm too hard? You do, don't you? I know what the kids tell you when I'm not around. They tell you how mean I am. Don't think I don't know it. It hurts too. I don't want my children to think of me as an ironhanded person who doesn't care. I do care. That's why I'm hard on them. If I have to be hard on the kids to teach them right from wrong, I'll do it. I don't want to, but I'll do it. You need to help me out too.

Wife: I know you care about the children.

Husband (sighs): I do. You think I need to loosen up on them, don't you? I want them to earn what they get, but I want them to know that I'm not such a rough guy. I'm really not.

• • • •

This man's wife could have reacted to her rigid husband in many ways. She could have berated him for his narrow-mindedness. She could have reasoned with him. She could have ignored him or given him a frosty look. Instead, she let him talk.

This wife looked beyond the behavior to the underlying emotions and motives. She tried to understand her husband's point of view. The responses she offered encouraged her husband to run through the full range of his emotions. She was wise in doing so, for as the man vented his feelings, he was able to direct himself. He concluded that his convictions were correct but that the method he used to enforce them needed an overhaul. His wife's soft responses loosened his rigid thoughts, making him open to more reasonable solutions.

Let's look at a different scenario, one involving a child. Children can be just as rigid as adults. We often try to force young people from their stiff stance, which, of course, usually helps the child's stubborn roots grow deeper. Note how a patient parental response softens the fear of a child, increasing the likelihood that she will follow the parent's leadership.

Girl: This is stupid. I don't want to do this.

Father: Do what? What don't you want to do?

Girl: Mom says I have to spend at least thirty minutes three days a week reading. This is my summer vacation. What does she expect me to do during my vacation? Read? Are you kidding? No way!

Father: You mean, you have other things in mind.

Girl: What do you think? I'm not going to read.

Father: And that's where the rub comes. I know Mom has told you that if you don't do what she tells you, she won't take you swimming. That's a problem.

Girl: Mom told me she wouldn't let me go swimming, but all the other kids' moms let their kids go. I don't want to sit in the house every day when my friends are at the pool!

Father: You'd think Mom was torturing you by making you read. It makes you so mad that you don't know what to do. I'm sure you've thought of ways around her rule.

Girl: Yeah, like I can really tell Mom what to do and then she'll let me have my way.

Father: Mom's not like that, is she? *(puts arm around daughter)* I trust you'll make wise choices. I know you're capable of it.

• • • •

This girl was afraid that her mother was inhibiting her freedom. Being self-absorbed, she wanted to do only the things *she* wanted to do—and nothing else—during her break from school. Her father wisely recognized that going toe to toe with his child over a family rule would only invite further trouble. Doing so would arouse the child's fear of losing control, resulting in further rigidity. He recognized that his daughter needed to express her feelings. Doing so would help her open up to other possibilities. He knew that she may end up challenging her mother's rule and may even have to receive a negative consequence. But to help her shed her rigid ways, she needed discipline *and* understanding.

JESUS AND RIGID PEOPLE

Jesus faced some of the most rigid people in Jewish society—the religious leaders. He refused to respond to them with the same inflexibility they showed. In the third chapter of John's Gospel, a Jewish leader named Nicodemus furtively sought Jesus' word in his search for ultimate truth. We can believe that Christ's tender way of dealing with people had led this man to want to know more about his way of life.

There are no guarantees that tenderness will result in change. Not all the people Jesus had contact with agreed with his way of life or espoused his teachings, but some did. And Jesus never varied from his loving approach to handling even the most rigid of people, even though at times he allowed other people to face the uncomfortable consequences of their own choices. By focusing on the relationship rather than achievement, Jesus softened the inflexibility of the people around him.

Summary: Sometimes the conflict we face in our families is the result of one person's rigidity, which often expresses itself in too many rules, harsh punishments, and control. Rigid behavior values compliance and emphasizes achievement over relationships, sin over grace. When we look beyond the rigidity, we often find a person who is afraid of losing control. When we respond to those feelings with understanding, we pave the way for the person to become more sensitive.

1. Place family relationships at the top of your priority list over the next few days. Consider the following suggestions as you draw family members closer to you:

- A hug, a handshake, or even a simple pat on the back connects one person's soul to another.
- When our behavior and words match, other people can trust us when we claim to want the best for them.
- Even though people may disagree, a show of understanding brings one person closer to another.
- The willingness to disclose feelings is a sign of strength, not weakness.
- Success is measured not necessarily by what we have accomplished but by our relationships.
- We prove that we accept ourselves when we can accept the differences in others.
- Family life depends on equality rather than superiority. God made us all equals.
- The answers to life are not so easily defined. We should never allow ourselves to believe we know them all.

2. If you find yourself struggling with rigid behavior with your spouse or children, ask yourself the following questions. Try to be aware of how you balance your behavior and emotions over the next few days. Notice

the difference it makes in how your family responds to you.

- Am I a stickler for rules? In what situations do I become very dogmatic and unyielding? How does my family react to me at those times?
- When I have stated my intentions and stuck to them, do I let anger get in my way? Do I discipline my kids or talk to my spouse with venom in my voice?
- After an argument, how quick am I to try to mend family relationships? Am I too quick? Am I not quick enough? What effect does my behavior have on the family?
- Does my family understand my motives? What can I do to promote understanding?
- What is the worst-case scenario if I loosen my standards for my children and spouse? How likely is it that those fears will be realized?

CHAPTER FIVE

Dependence: Struggling for Independence

DARLA Yount glared at her mother with a look that hurt worse than a physical blow. The child's eyes were redder than they should have been. Her eyebrows were pulled tightly inward. Hard wrinkles gripped her forehead. Her fists were clenched, although the girl was hardly aware of it. All she knew was that she was mad. She was mad at her mother for suggesting that she did not know how far to go in her relationships with boys.

Moments earlier, Darla's mom had told her that she was not to talk with her boyfriend anymore that night. Darla took offense at the rule and confronted her mother with the absurdity of her demand.

"Who do you think you are, telling me who I can and can't talk to? I'll decide that, and nobody else!" the girl had retorted.

Darla's mom finally succeeded in persuading her

daughter to hang up the phone. Trying to reason with her, she explained, "Darla, it's not healthy for you to be so attached to a boy at your age. You're too young for that sort of thing. Believe me, I know what I'm talking about." The mother tried to stay composed as she talked, but inwardly she was anything but calm.

As too many of their conversations were prone to do, this one quickly got out of hand. Taking the offensive, Darla demanded, "What do you know about me and Aaron? You don't know anything about us! How can you possibly sit there and tell me it's too thick between us?"

Almost pleading with her stubborn child, the mother replied, "Darla, you've got this way about you that says 'Come and get me.' I see it, and I know Aaron sees it. There's no telling what might happen between the two of you. I only know that when a girl calls a boy as much as you do Aaron, she's asking for trouble."

Indignant, Darla shot back, "What do you mean by that? You mean you think Aaron and I are going to have sex?"

"Darla!"

"Admit it. That's what you're talking about. Oh, that's just great! Wait until my friends hear about this one. I've got a boyfriend, and my mother thinks I'm about to get pregnant."

"I'm just saying that at age eleven, you don't need a boyfriend. You'll have plenty of time for that when you're older."

An hour passed. Darla remained in her bedroom, refusing to venture into the living room, where the rest of her family sat. Though still upset over her argument with her mother, she had cooled off somewhat. It seemed that her mind was playing tricks on her. One moment she thought, "I'll never forgive my mother for talking to me like that." The next moment a softer side of her mused, "Maybe Mom's right. I don't want to grow up yet. I need to apologize to her."

Worn out from thinking, Darla determined to shut off her thoughts. She was confused, and besides that, she hated to be angry. But her mind would not cooperate. Persistent thoughts ran randomly through her head, alternately goading her to rebel against her mother and encouraging her to accept her mom's counsel.

Simultaneously, Darla's mom struggled to control her own thoughts. Speaking to her husband but to herself as well, she worried aloud, "Maybe I was too hard on Darla. She's just excited that a boy is showing her some attention. I remember what that was like." Then abruptly shifting emotional gears, her voice hardened as she added, "But I'm not going to let her make the same mistakes I made when I was young. I wasn't strong enough to be myself. I *had* to have a boyfriend. I learned some lessons about life the hard way, and I don't want Darla to have to go through what I did. She's just like me."

Her husband mechanically listened to her as she talked, but she knew she was not getting through to him. He did not understand. It seemed he could not fathom the depth of her feelings. Sighing, she stuck her head back in the magazine she was reading, even though the words she read were little more than a blur on the page.

WHAT IS DEPENDENCE?

In the past decade, pop psychologists have convinced us that to be dependent is to be inadequate. They fastened terms such as *enabler, codependent, weakling, push-over,* and worse to this term. We have been inundated with books, magazine articles, and media stories convincing us that dependence is dysfunctional.

Is it?

Darla's story depicts a girl who wants to make friends with a boy. She is outgoing and quickly attaches to others. She is concerned about her friends and family alike. She merely acts on her urges to get involved with others. Not a particularly condemning set of characteristics when you examine them at face value.

Mrs. Yount's concern for her child results from her own youthful experiences. As a teenager she had more boyfriends than she could count. And her heart was broken more often than it should have been. She knew what it meant to be dependent on others for happiness. She paid a stiff price for her poor judgment and did not want to see her daughter whirled through life's wringer as she had been. Her response to Darla's situation is understanding, even compassionate.

Dependence need not be a negative word. The old saying "No man is an island" reminds us that we all live in a world that demands cooperation and interdependence. God made people for relationships. The relations found in the home are meant to mirror the ones God desires for all his children. Husbands and wives are to strengthen one another, each drawing on the other for support and affection. Children need parental discipline and affirmation so that their self-concept will be positive. Every family member has a role. No person can be a family alone. It takes people working together to build this unique unit. Dependence is necessary for family success.

However, dependence can also be unhealthy. Consider the following examples of how imbalanced dependence can wreak havoc on family members:

- A wife who has not worked in ten years is itching to get back into her profession. She knows she can arrange for satisfactory after-school care for her kids, and the family could use the additional income. What's more, she has a good lead on a promising job. Her husband opposes the idea, though, believing that a woman's place is in the home. Knowing that she would only stir the waters by broaching the subject with her husband, this wife keeps quiet, mentioning neither her desires nor possibilities to her husband.

- A six-year-old boy's parents worried about him. While they were glad that their son liked to be with them, they were worried that he could do nothing apart from them. It wasn't bad that he insisted that his friends play at his house rather than at theirs. But he was now in school and had to be away from home every day. The disagreeable thought of being away from his parents was more than the boy could stand. He hated school. His teachers did all they could to coax him to participate in normal classroom activities. His parents felt guilty each morning as they sent their forlorn child off to school.

- Fifteen-year-old Julia had one close friend. Julia and Roxie had been tight pals for five years. However, in the past few months, Roxie had become more mobile. She had grown closer to a girl who could drive and who had more boyfriends than Julia did. Julia wanted to be as outgoing as her friend but did not have it in her to assert herself the way Roxie did. Roxie kiddingly called Julia a snob. Though Julia went along with her friend's ribbing, she wondered if maybe Roxie was right.

• A businessman who seemed confident and successful only sheepishly admitted to feeling inadequate in social settings. He confided, "My wife is a lot better than I am at that sort of thing. I'm not one for chit-chat." Though he attended the obligatory functions, no one but his wife and closest friends knew how much he agonized over these events.

THE MANY FACES OF DEPENDENCE

Dependence shows itself in nearly all family members. Whether this trait takes the form of an overly passive wife, a clinging child, an unassertive teenager, or an insecure husband, it defines some aspect of every person's behavior. Some people think of dependence as an exclusively female characteristic, but males can be just as dependent.

When dependence becomes exaggerated, relationship problems crop up. Look at the following ways dependence can be inappropriate:

Dependence Results in Overworked Sensitivity

Sensitivity can be both a blessing and a curse, depending on how it is expressed. Without it, family relationships quickly harden. With too much of it, though, family relationships may be wrenched apart. Interestingly, many women complain that their husbands don't express enough sensitivity. Men, on the other hand, often wish their wives were tougher and less emotional. Many men and women push their personal agenda on their children with statements like, "Big boys don't cry" or, "Girls cry about everything." Actually, neither statement is true. Big boys *do* cry, and girls *don't* cry about everything. Yet these stereotypes have had an impact on both males and females. In many ways, our societal expectations prevent each sex from striking that healthy balance of sensitivity.

Curiously, our society sees overworked sensitivity as a greater problem than underdeveloped sensitivity. Overly sensitive people are fingered as disturbed or dysfunctional because they

- experience hurt feelings over seemingly insignificant matters
- read too much into the statements and actions of others
- worry excessively about matters that are beyond their control
- expect the worst to happen
- assume that others are more upset than they really are
- frequently feel overwhelmed with emotions that are hard to control

Imbalanced sensitivity often signals a need for *selfishness*. That's right—selfishness! Sensitive people often take care of everyone but themselves, giving to the point of emotional exhaustion. They can bring balance to their lives by looking out for their personal needs in addition to the needs of others. When their own emotional bucket is full, they can interact more effectively with other family members.

Dependence Tries to Force Solutions

We all want what is best for the family. That yearning is simply natural. Dependence, though, can push a family member to want so badly to make things right that the opposite happens—family life becomes even more tangled! Some family counselors use the term *enmeshment* to describe the way family members become so absorbed in each others' lives that they lose their objectivity. These people often try to force solutions to family problems by

- giving streams of unsolicited opinions or advice
- being so sympathetic that others take advantage of that forgiving spirit
- refusing to let others face the consequences of their own mistakes
- feeling responsible for making others happy
- experiencing guilt when others blunder, as if it were a personal failure
- becoming excessively invested in others' feelings and emotions
- yelling and screaming to make a point

If we are to maintain family unity, we must learn to practice healthy separation. We can start by trusting that others can figure out how they will manage personal dilemmas. As family leaders, we should be helpers rather than taskmasters.

Parents can teach children to be independent by maintaining a healthy distance from the children's daily crises. Spouses can be effective partners as they assist each other without trying to force their will on family and personal matters. Note how we can provide independent-minded leadership to our families. We can

- offer opinions when asked, but not when they will lead to further misunderstanding

- show forgiveness while also allowing others to be accountable for mistakes
- let others experience the natural consequences of their choices
- listen to others without acting on the urge to give lectures or sermons
- realize that excessive emotional investment may stunt others' personal growth
- give others the responsibility for drawing conclusions about their need for change

Dependence Relies Too Heavily on Recognition

We all need recognition. It gives us a feeling of importance, of belonging, of self-worth. In fact, we need recognition not only from others but also from within ourselves. Dependence can make us rely so heavily on other people's approval that life seems empty without it. For example, a child is almost constantly disruptive. In a rare introspective moment, he explains, "If I don't act bad, my daddy won't even notice me."

A wife complains to a friend, "I used to have so much more confidence in myself than I do now. I think if my husband would only spend more time with me, I could regain the poise I used to have."

A workaholic father talks constantly about how busy he is. He mutters that he does not have the time it takes to complete just one day's work. He hopes his wife and children will be proud to have such an important man around the house.

Our worth as people should not rest solely on other people's attention. It must start within the individual. All family members are creations of God, with stature and prestige born within them. Parents who help children feel good about themselves, faults and all, encourage a healthy balance between dependence and independence. Husbands and wives need affirmation from others, but they first should claim the significance that comes from simply being one of God's prized creations.

Dependence Denies Personal Needs

A Christian woman who struggled with dependence once told me, "The Bible says that I should deny myself if I want to be a true follower of Christ. After all, that's what Christ himself did and encouraged us to do. But I'll be honest with you, I'm so exhausted from taking care of my family that I'm not sure I agree with what the Bible says." A look of horror shot across her face as she realized what she had said. She quickly added, "I don't mean that I disagree with anything Jesus taught. It's just that I'm confused with how far to take that advice."

Even though Jesus inspired his followers to take on the servant role, he certainly had no intention of promoting a one-sided approach to life's relationships. He took time to rest, allowed others to tend to his needs, and even assented to others' indulgence of him. No doubt, Jesus' life and teachings were meant to help people strike a balance in relationships.

Yet dependence may convince a person to disregard personal needs. A dependent person may

- ignore obvious signs of burnout, choosing instead to plod ahead
- console others, but deny the personal need for emotional comfort
- refuse the help of others, not wanting to be a burden

- stuff uncomfortable feelings inside to the point of developing psychosomatic illness

People who see personal need as a sign of weakness are out of balance. They must learn that it is necessary to assert their needs when the situation calls for it, do things their way from time to time, take time for personal relaxation, and occasionally take an uncharacteristic risk.

Listen to the comments of dependent family members who have learned that it is healthy to balance personal need with the needs of others:

Teenager: I used to hate to say no to people because I was afraid they'd get mad at me. But I realize that I have to be my own person, no matter what others might think.

Husband: My wife and I do things differently. I've quit trying to make her do everything the way I would do it. Funny thing, now she asks for my opinion more than ever.

Mother: I don't want to punish my children. That's the worst part of being a parent. But if I don't, they'll never learn to be responsible to anyone other than themselves. I'm doing the right thing by being firm with them.

WHAT MESSAGE LIES BENEATH DEPENDENCE?
Perhaps more than any other demand, the dependent family member is trying to satisfy the need for personal comfort. By becoming overly involved in family con-

flicts, the person is saying, "I feel distressed when this family disagrees over anything. When another family member hurts, I hurt. I can't stand the pain!"

As I talk with family members about their dependent behavior, I hear interesting comments that explain why dependency chokes their family.

> *Mother:* When I was a child, my parents constantly fought with each other. I recall telling my sister that when I had my own family, we would not treat each other the way our parents treated our family. My children don't understand why I tell them over and over that they need to talk nicely to each other. They look at me as if I am crazy. I'm not. I just don't want them to experience what I did.

The mother's aim was positive, but she created an imbalance in her family. Her rule, "Don't express your real opinions," served her well as a child; to have told her parents what she thought would have resulted in yet another fight. However, that same rule didn't apply to her children. It served only to create a void in their family communication.

> *Husband:* I'm not dependent. I'm my own person, and my family knows that. My task is to bring home the bacon. If I provide for my family the way a man should, then I've done my job. All I care to hear is an occasional thank-you from my wife and kids.

In his desire to become completely independent of his family, this man sent a message about his need to feel valued. Imagine the loneliness he would experience if his wife and children took him up on his wish to be a self-contained man. Whether or not he realized it, the imbalance of this husband's emotions left him depending on others to assure him of his worth as a person. His need for approval is one all family members share. The shame of it is that it's not necessary for family members to prove themselves worthy. In a healthy family, family members have worth simply because they are human.

It is hard for us to comprehend fully the importance other family members play in defining our personal sense of worth. Every family member needs the others. In a dependent family, balance is missing. Through disproportionate behaviors, emotional needs are communicated to others. But when such elements as the freedom to feel unconditional acceptance, tolerance of differing views, and honest expression are in place in the home, dependence can be balanced. When these elements are lacking, the result is predictable: The family becomes entangled in a web of emotions, and each family member searches for a way out.

BRING BALANCE TO DEPENDENCE

A mother felt some confusion about family matters. She was not getting the response she believed she deserved from her husband and two children. She found herself griping at the kids more than she would have liked, and she felt that her husband was not giving her the support she needed. She asked the family to confer with her one evening to discuss the problem. Through their discussion, she learned that she had more control over the effectiveness of her leadership than she realized. Note how she learned from the feedback she sought from her family:

Mother: Things haven't been going as well around here as I'd like. We need to talk about some things.

Father: Like what?

Mother (turns to children): Like the way I haven't been getting any respect around here. You two ignore me whenever I ask you to do anything. I had to scream at you this afternoon to get you to clean your rooms.

Seven-year-old son: It wasn't that dirty. I was going to do it later.

Mother: But that's what you always say. You tell me you're going to do it later, but then it never happens. And, Jackie, you're just as bad. You act as if I've put you in jail when I ask you to do anything. And then when Dad comes home, both of you tattle to him and cause a big scene. We could stop all this nonsense if you would just mind me.

Eight-year-old daughter: But, Mom, when do we get to do what *we* want to do?

Mother: Are you kidding? You do what you want all day long. I do everything I can to make sure you kids are happy. I would like some respect in return.

Father: Maybe that's the problem. You try too hard to make the kids happy. They take advantage of it.

• • • •

From there, the family talked of the reasons for their chronic discord. Though the children denied that they received too much latitude from their mother, she became convinced that she had become too weak. Her husband was right. She made too much of an effort to put the kids' wishes before their need for responsibility. Her own imbalanced dependence dictated the kind of mother she was. Conversely, she was inadvertently fostering imbalanced dependence in her children. Later, after the children were in bed, the husband and wife talked further.

> *Mother:* Jim, do you really think I'm too soft on the kids?
>
> *Father:* To be honest—yes. They know you hate to discipline them, so they take you as far as they can before they finally do what they're supposed to.
>
> *Mother:* That doesn't make sense to me. I never did that to my parents.
>
> *Father:* Maybe you're different from the kids.
>
> *Mother:* So what am I supposed to do—*force* them to obey me? I've tried that, and it doesn't work.
>
> *Father:* Maybe you don't need to force them. Maybe you could be less emotional. You get upset pretty easily, you know.

Mother: Me be less emotional? That would be hard. *(laughs)* I'm Italian. I can't be anything but emotional!

Father: That's what I like about you. It's great that you're so sensitive. It's just that when you get involved with the kids, or with me for that matter, sometimes you come on so strong you lose your effectiveness.

••••

Summary: Family conflict can arise when people are overly dependent on each other. Family members show unhealthy dependence when they are overly sensitive, when they try to force solutions to problems, when they rely too heavily on other people's recognition of them, and when they deny their personal needs. We must remember that the message behind dependent behavior is an overstatement of unmet individual needs. When we recognize the behavior and understand its message, we can respond with understanding, which will promote growth in the whole family.

1. If you as parents are overly dependent, place yourself in the shoes of each family member and ask, What does that family member think of me? Why?

2. Carefully observe the conversations you have with each family member. Notice the reaction you get when you become overly involved in a problem. See if the family member tries to shift responsibility to you. Conversely, notice what happens when you state the boundaries and then refuse to force a solution.

3. Be bluntly honest with yourself as you examine why you act as you do toward your family. Does your family understand your good intentions? If not, what behavior blocks them?

4. How can you be selfish in a way that benefits both you and your family?

5. If your children are overly dependent, take the following steps to help them effectively balance their emotions. First, step back from your children's situations; then objectively identify their real needs. Do they need you to be decisive? Do they need to learn from their mistakes? Do they need time to figure things out?

6. Plan a conversation with your children. Try to avoid

giving advice, opinions, or suggestions. Let this be a time for them to express themselves.

7. When you talk with your children, use phrases such as "That's something you can do" or "You can do that by yourself." Get out of the role of protecting sensitive children.

8. Give your children simple chores to complete. Your objective is to instill a sense of responsibility in them. Help them learn that they can act independently.

9. Take the opportunity to point out the little things your children are doing right. Daily do something that will build their self-esteem.

10. As you lead your family, take notes on the ways you can practice healthy independence and simultaneously teach other family members to do the same. You might write a list of guidelines you intend to follow. Here is a start to your list:

- Give advice to others sparingly, only when it seems that they will accept it.
- Look at yourself as a team member, not as the one who must take all the responsibility.
- Recognize that change takes place slowly. Show patience accordingly.
- Set your emotions aside when you must make tough decisions.
- Accept setbacks as an inevitable part of family growth.

- Tell your spouse and children that it is truly okay if they disagree with you.

11. Make a conscious effort to evaluate your parenting style over the next few days. If you are a parent who tends to be dependent in relationships, work on being more assertive. If you go too far in the other direction, work on balancing your need to depend on others. Here are some questions you can ask yourself as you go through this self-study:

- How have the events of the past affected the way you act toward your children?
- What messages about yourself do you send to your children through the way you react to their mistakes?
- In what ways do you foster dependence in your children?
- In what ways do you try to hide your real feelings from your children? How aware are they of your emotions?
- What in your children's actions and speech suggests they are modeling your behavior?
- Is the general mood in your home happy? depressed? anxious? hopeful?
- How do you handle sticky emotional situations? Do you try to sweep bad feelings under the rug? deal with them openly? make all the decisions?

CHAPTER SIX

Argumentativeness: Winning at All Cost

THE door slammed as Shanna, Ted, and their mother, Carrie, flew into the house. Instantly, the kitchen was transformed into a battlefield as the fight that had erupted in the car spilled over into the house.

Livid at her insolent son, Carrie barked, "How many times do I have to tell you to quit calling your Aunt Cathy and hanging up on her? She's busy. Quit irritating her. That's so childish of you!"

Upset to the point of tears, Ted repeated what he had tried to tell his mother when she first accused him: "Mother, I didn't call Aunt Cathy! Believe me. I didn't do it! Why do you always believe her instead of me? What makes her so right all the time? You and Aunt Cathy are just alike. You never believe a word anybody says!"

"That's not true," his mother defended herself.

"When you tell the truth, I believe you. But I know when you're lying and when you're not."

Finishing his mother's implied thought, Ted mockingly asked, "You mean you believe Aunt Cathy over me? You think I'm lying, don't you?"

Trying to explain herself, Carrie snapped, "Let's just say I know what I'm talking about. You don't need to know all the details. I know more than you think."

Itching to enter the fray, Shanna defended her brother, asserting, "Mother, Aunt Cathy doesn't know half of what she thinks she does. She just tries to get you to run this family the way she runs hers, and she doesn't know what she's doing."

Indignant that her daughter would speak so disrespectfully about her own relative, Carrie snapped her fingers and shouted, "You can go straight to your room! I'm not going to listen to that kind of sass from a child who thinks she knows everything. Young lady, you can just forget about television tonight!"

As Shanna stomped to the rear of the house toward her bedroom, she passed her father, who wore a sick expression of disgust on his face. Almost afraid to ask, he stopped cold in his tracks and posed the predictable question: "What's going on in there? What's all the fuss about?"

Not bothering to break her stride, Shanna answered her father in a voice loud enough to reach her mother, "Mother's in there accusing us of doing things to Aunt Cathy when the whole problem is that Aunt Cathy always sticks her nose where it doesn't belong."

"Brother," Dad mumbled as he haltingly trekked toward the kitchen. He figured he should do what he could to settle his family down, but he certainly didn't look forward to the task ahead of him.

Hoping to sound authoritative, Art's voice instinctively became deeper as he demanded, "What's going on in here?"

"Butt out of this! These two disrespectful juveniles have been prank calling Cathy, but they won't admit to it. I can't stand the way they treat her and then lie to me about it as if it's no big deal."

Simultaneously, Ted protested his mother's put-down as his dad defended his intent merely to squelch a quarrel that had obviously gotten out of hand. Not caring that she was supposed to be sequestered in her room, Shanna reappeared and joined in the now-frenzied kitchen brawl. Had this scene been played before a television audience, it might have been humorous, it was so skewed. Unfortunately, this fight was the real thing. Within minutes the verbal fisticuffs ended, but the family spent the rest of the night licking its sore wounds.

The kind of unresolved fighting this family experienced leaves everyone drained. No one wins. Everyone retreats to a corner to stew and plan counterattacks.

While most of us enjoy a good argument, very few of us like the argumentativeness that can put a stranglehold on our families. What can we do when one or more of our family members show a pattern of argumentative behavior?

ARGUMENTATIVENESS HAS ANGRY ROOTS
We tend to think that arguments and anger go hand in hand. After all, an argument is an exaggerated form of

communication just as anger is an exaggerated emotion. Right?

Well, almost. As we have said in earlier chapters, anger is not always bad. Remember that all emotions are valid because God has given them to us. We express every emotion, even if we don't express them verbally. Family members who feel misunderstood will use their behavior to communicate their thoughts and feelings to others.

However, we must admit that because we so readily see anger as argumentativeness, it has gained an unhealthy reputation. Anger does not destroy relationships. The *misuse* of anger cripples family relationships.

As we return to the scenario above, we see that each family member brought a personal set of emotional baggage to the argument. The mother was irritated that her children had been disrespectful to her sister. Nothing is wrong with that feeling; parents should expect their children to honor others. Ted felt his mother had falsely accused him of foul play and hoped to defend himself. Shanna wanted to throw in her opinion about Aunt Cathy's intrusive ways. If we view the situation independently, we cannot argue with these kids' feelings. They are valid. And we certainly cannot blame the dad for his part in the fracas. He tried to bring peace back into the home.

Where did this family go wrong? How can four people, all of whom have valid feelings, become hopelessly hooked into an emotional slugfest that took the family nowhere but down?

Anger was misused.

Argumentativeness in the home is frequently a result of misplaced anger. The feelings underlying the fight have been misused. When argumentative people take the time to explain their behavior, other people may understand their rationale for being upset. Too often, though, argumentative family members are so convicted by their emotions that they fail to see how anger gets in the way.

In the following scenarios we can see five ways we misuse anger: sarcasm, verbal explosions, threats, blame, and obnoxious behavior.

Sarcasm

> **Son to mother:** You think you're the best mother in the world. You sit around and tell your friends what a wonderful parent you are. When you and that lady down the street get together, you love to talk about which one has the worst child. I can just hear you say *(mockingly),* "Oh, you don't know what it's like to live with a child as strong willed as my little Henry." It makes me sick to think about it.

> **Wife to husband:** Where are you when I need help with the kids? You claim you've got work to do at the office. I honestly believe that you men stay late so you don't have to come home and face the music. You probably spend your time playing computer games. I know you're not working!

Verbal Explosions

> **Father to rebellious son:** That's it! I've had it with your smart talk! Get out! Do you hear me? I said leave! Go to your room! Go outside! I don't care where you go; just get away from me!

Daughter to mother: I hate living in this house! I hate it! I wish everyone in this family would die and I could start all over with a new family! I don't ever want to look at any of you again for the rest of my life!

Threats

Mother to son: I'm going to tell you something, and I want you to listen because you need to hear this. If you keep acting up, you'll never get out of high school. You'll wind up in the juvenile detention center. And don't you even think that I'll come down there to visit you, because I won't.

Daughter to mom: Mom, do you realize what's going to happen if you keep spoiling Jeremy? He's going to be so wild when he's a teenager that no one will be able to stop him. I can promise you that's the way it's going to be. I've seen it happen to too many of my friends.

Blame

Husband to wife: The main problem around here is that you're so wishy-washy. You say one thing to the kids and then let them talk you out of it. Of course they're going to run over you. They know they've got you!

Brother to sister: I hate it when you tell Mom and Dad everything I do. What difference does it make if they don't know every little detail about my life?

If you would just quit sticking your nose into my business, my life would be a whole lot simpler.

Obnoxious Behavior

Father (pointing his finger at his son): If you think you can talk to me like that and get away with it, you've got another think coming. There's a word for people like you. It's *punk*. Did you know you're acting like a punk? Well, you are! And I plan to show you that punks don't rule this house! Nice people do!

Sister to younger sister: You haven't heard the last of me. Tomorrow I've got plenty to tell all your friends at school. We'll see what they think of you once I get through telling them what you're really like. If you think you can treat me the way you do and then sit back while I just take it, you're wrong!

CHANGE FAMILY ARGUMENTS TO PRODUCTIVE DIALOGUE

Is it any wonder anger and arguments are such close companions? The misuse of anger is probably the chief trait of argumentative people.

Used appropriately, family arguments can be transformed into productive dialogue. Rather than preach a don't-be-angry message to your family, consider sending this message: If you must be angry, use this emotion correctly. Don't drift into unnecessary arguments.

Family leaders who want to control anger in their families need to consider two levels of learning. The first involves learning how to handle your own anger;

the second deals with learning how to handle your family members' anger.

Handling Your Own Anger

Several basic principles can help you control your own anger.

Keep problem situations in perspective. In his letter to the Ephesians, the apostle Paul writes, "'In your anger do not sin': Do not let the sun go down while you are still angry" (Ephesians 4:26). When Paul speaks of bitterness, he is referring to anger that turns into poison. Unresolved anger tends to simmer inside to the point that it becomes a burden rather than a positive force. Instead of wishing that anger would disappear altogether, we should recognize its inevitability and face it head-on. For example, a mother is irritated at her child's forgetfulness. To make matters worse, her husband frequently makes excuses for their child's irresponsibility. By brooding over the situation, this mother may find herself griping and complaining to her family, desperately hoping to change their ways. But by keeping her feelings in perspective, she will consistently follow up on her child's mistakes, doing what she can to make family life consistent and predictable. Her influence over both her child and her husband will be stronger as she correctly asserts herself.

Stay in control of yourself. A sobering fact is that the only person I can control is me, and the only person you can control is you. Argumentative people often try to control others, sometimes almost forcefully. While power tactics may temporarily douse burning family fires, they do not cool anger's embers. By putting the brakes on anger before it screeches out of control, family leaders can increase their influence over others. For example, a husband is upset at his wife for unnecessarily arguing with their daughter. His knee-jerk impulse is to yell at his wife for her abrasive behavior. But, instead of letting his anger spill out, he patiently listens as his wife rants and raves about their daughter's senseless conduct. After his wife has emptied her emotional bucket, she sighs and asks, "Have you got any suggestions for handling the situation differently?" The husband realizes he has acted wisely by withholding his own angry feelings. By showing constraint over his own emotions, he shows his wife that she can look to him as a resource for strength and encouragement.

Stick to the subject. When we argue, we want to build as strong a case as possible for our point of view. Hence, when we attack a problem, we search for as many weapons as we can find. Emotional darts such as poisonous talk, condemning remarks, taunting words, or dredging up the past make our verbal assault tough to withstand, but they do little to resolve family problems. The apostle Paul implies that we are to fight fairly when he states, "Get rid of all bitterness, rage and anger, brawling and slander, along with every form of malice" (Ephesians 4:31). For example, a boy is upset that his parents have made him clean his room before they will allow him to have a friend spend the night with him. The boy reluctantly does what he is told but gives only a halfhearted effort. When he claims he is through with his task, his mother inspects his room and concludes that he needs to do more work before she will give her seal of approval. He complains and accuses his mother of being unreasonably strict. Tempted to level her son with a few choice words, this mother wisely refrains. She simply sticks to the issue: He must clean his room before he gets to do what he wants. Seeing that he cannot engage his mother in a war of words, the boy complies.

Handling Your Family Members' Anger

By controlling your own argumentative tendencies, you have won half the battle over anger. The other half of the battle is to help other family members stay away from damaging emotional brawls. Three principles can help you handle your family members' anger.

Listen for anger's message. Because anger is so often misused, it tends to threaten, hurt, irritate, or provoke us. But before we react in these negative ways, remember: There is a reason for every behavior. Learn to look beneath angry behavior to the message the family member is trying to communicate. Hard as it is to do, the wise family member asks the question, What are you trying to tell me through your behavior? By correctly reading the message behind argumentative behavior, we can take the wind out of the sails of the anger. The anger is more likely to subside and give way to reason. For example, a daughter comes home and loudly complains, "I hate going to that school! There's nothing you can do to make me try anymore. Either we move to another school district or I quit!"

Rather than engage in a war of words with her distraught daughter, her mother looks for the underlying message and comments, "Things must not have gone well today. You look exhausted." Taking her mother's remark as a positive sign, the girl goes on to express her frustration. An argument over the child's ridiculous demand is avoided.

Wait for the right time. Wait until right time to debate. One key ingredient for a good argument is poor timing of constructive criticism. When family members voice their disgust, hurt, irritation, or disapproval, we often want to make things right. Thus, we offer our two cents' worth of advice, hoping it will be taken in the same constructive spirit in which it is being offered. The quick shift from complaint to argument tells us that words alone will not solve a problem. We must let time work its magic before we provide the direct wisdom and guidance that is needed. For example, a father is in a stew because things at work have not gone smoothly. He takes his feelings out on his family, first complaining that he does not like the supper his wife served, then demanding that the kids pipe down while he watches television. His wife and children talk privately and argue over who gets to choke him first. Wisdom prevails, and the family agrees that to confront him while he is in a foul mood will only make his disposition worse. The next morning, when the father seems less tense, his family tactfully tells him that his mood from the previous night put the rest of the family in an awkward spot. They explain that they should not have borne the brunt of his frustrations. He apologizes and agrees that he will try to be more pleasant when he comes home that night.

Persist. One reason argumentative people continue their verbal onslaught is that experience has taught them that others will compromise just to keep peace in the home. While I am certainly in favor of flexibility in family decisions, softness in the face of argumentative demands ensures one thing: more arguments. Stating guidelines and sticking to them erases the argumentative person's hope that his or her tactics will be fruitful. For example, a teenager's friends talk him into staying out later than his prescribed curfew. When he comes in thirty minutes late, he offers his parents a lame excuse. Deciding to let their actions speak louder than their words, the parents tell the youth that he must come in thirty minutes early the following weekend. The boy protests, but he does not succeed in changing his parents' rule. Deciding that his parents are resolute, the teen turns down his friends the next time they suggest he test his parents' rules.

ESTABLISH A POSITIVE TONE

An older friend of mine once gave me a tour of his vegetable garden. As he showed off the fruits (vegetables?) of his labor, he continually reminded me that proper watering and fertilizing were needed to get the results he got. At one point, the elderly man turned to me and said, "Actually, growing a garden is a lot like raising a family. You've got to give it the right climate to grow."

In squelching argumentativeness in the home, I have found that the emotional climate is every bit as important a discipline tool as reward and punishments. A task of the family leader is to set an atmosphere ripe for growth and then trust that the children will flourish. Following are three leadership qualities that set the tone for growth and diminish the likelihood that arguments will strangle the home.

Effective Family Leaders Must Refuse to Judge
One of the more difficult tricks of family life is simultaneously to hold an opinion and refrain from passing

judgment on others whose opinion differs. Parents may believe that boys who wear an earring look tacky. But if a boy with an earring comes into their home, parents may have difficulty keeping their opinion from negatively influencing their reaction to that young person. The combination of a strongly held opinion and quick judgment is sure to increase the chances of arguments.

A girl explained to me the reason for her frequent arguments with her parents. She said, "I have my opinions, and my parents have theirs. I don't like the way they think, and they don't like the way I think. They try to change my mind, while I try to change theirs. Neither one of us ever wins." I might add that this astute girl was ten years old. Barely into double digits in age, she had already figured out that argumentativeness is too often a match of stubborn wills.

I asked this girl what her reaction would be if she stated her opinion and her parents simply said, "We understand how you think, although we see things differently."

Her quick response was, "I'd faint."

Too often we fear that by refraining from pronouncing judgment against something we believe is wrong, we are tacitly giving our approval. Yet this fear is generally unfounded. Kids know their parents well and are fully aware of their parents' stance on family issues. I asked this ten-year-old girl how she would feel if her parents kept their differing opinions to themselves. Her insightful response was, "Oh, that would be great! I know what they think. I just don't want to be put down!"

Argumentativeness is typically a defensive maneuver. In a family climate that takes away the need to defend against an onslaught of opposing views, harmony flourishes.

Effective Family Leaders Must Be Responsive

When family members give reasons for their arguments, they typically say such things as

- "I don't like it when they try to force me to be them."
- "I feel so frustrated when they don't listen to me."
- "They're trying to take responsibilities away from me."
- "I hate being analyzed."
- "No one understands."

The common thread in each of these statements is *I want a response to my needs*. An argumentative father and husband bluntly explained, "I simply want to be heard."

A vicious cycle occurs in argumentative families. It goes something like this: A woman finds herself with a dilemma. She feels discouraged. To alleviate those nagging feelings of despair, she seeks a positive response from someone. She simply wants to be told, "You are an okay person. There's hope for escaping your struggle." However, instead of gaining empathetic understanding, her family members try to diagnose her problem and evaluate her decision-making ability. Tension rises. The woman seeks to release that tension. If her family members don't respond with understanding, confusion sets in. Feeling more desperate, she restates her needs in a combative way, hoping against reasonable hope to get the response she needs.

Finally her husband stops the cycle. He says to her, "Honey, you've had some rough days. At first I thought that it was my job to help you solve your problems, but you seem to get even more upset. I finally realized that was not the right approach. How can I help you? Tell me what the last few days have been like for you." The husband's response to his wife's emotional need calmed her argumentativeness. Nothing relaxes tension more than being heard. Guilt and its emotional cousin despair are chased away by well-placed affection, a touch, or a simple nod of the head. Responsiveness uncovers frightening feelings. It feels good. It dispels the need to argue.

Effective Family Leaders Make Honesty Easy

Ask children from an argumentative home why they refused to tell the truth the first time they were asked. You might hear, "Are you kidding? And risk getting grounded for the rest of the week? No way!"

Pose the same question to a mother who has shut herself off from her children. She might say, "Ha! The last time I tried to open up to my kids, they tore into me. I vowed to myself then that I would never again put myself in that position!"

A husband who is anything but open with his wife might reveal, "I have my own private world. I plan to keep it that way. If my wife knew everything I thought, she would probably divorce me on the spot."

In argumentative homes, it is risky to be completely open with other family members. That need to hide from others invites loneliness.

But once people become convinced that they can safely take the risk of exposing their feelings, they will replace their deceitful, argumentative habits with honest communication.

In families made safe by leaders who are willing to listen and express understanding, parents and adults are free to be themselves. A child in this kind of family may say, "I did something wrong, but it's no big deal. My parents will listen to the circumstances and try to understand. They always do. That doesn't mean I won't get punished, but I know they will listen first."

A mother who has taught this quality to her children may comment, "I can shoot straight with the kids. They know I want what's best for them."

A husband may say of his wife, "I don't need to hide myself from her. She knows I'm not perfect, and she accepts that fact. I feel as if I've improved through the years simply because she takes the time to look deep inside me."

Summary: Argumentativeness can destroy family harmony. As family leaders try to lessen the tension in their homes, they must seek to control their own anger and to help other family members with their argumentativeness. As family leaders look beneath the argumentative behavior to the messages family members are trying to communicate, they create an atmosphere that promotes the open exchange of ideas and family unity.

1. Call a family conference. Explain that no one is in trouble and that this is not a time for family members to complain or fuss at one another. Hold an open discussion about the way your family handles disagreements. You might want to use the following questions as guidelines for your dialogue:

- What do we hope to accomplish when we argue with one another?
- What do we sacrifice when we argue?
- How do each of us show anger?
- What is unique about the way we become upset?
- How do we feel about ourselves?
- How does the way we treat each other reflect our personal self-esteem?
- What can we do to give each other an emotional boost?
- When one family member has a bad day, how does it affect the rest of us?

2. In the next week, observe your conversations with each family member. If you can keep track of the ratio of negative to positive comments you make, do so. You might keep a score of yourself at fifteen-minute intervals. As a learning experience, ask yourself the following questions:

- Did that family member seem to feel that it is safe to discuss personal matters with me?
- What did I do and say to make it easy or difficult for him or her to talk openly with me?
- How freely did I offer my opinions?
- Were my opinions welcome?
- Did I stop communication or cause an argument by being too quick to judge?
- What do I feel when a family member says or does things that I disagree with?
- Am I accepting of the disagreement?
- Do I become physically tense? embarrassed? angry? panicked? worried? composed? frustrated? calm?
- Did my gestures match my statements?
- Was I completely honest with my family member, or did I hide certain thoughts and feelings?
- How hard did I push to get my point across?
- Were my efforts effective?
- What can I learn from the response I received?

CHAPTER SEVEN

Withdrawal: Playing It Safe

WHEN anyone mentions the word *withdrawal,* what characteristics come to mind?

seclusion	withholding	stubborn
isolation	distrustful	uncommunicative
retreat	anxious	detached
sensitive	timid	inhibited

Mention the word *argumentative* and the mental picture it paints is more lively.

ornery	conflict	haggle
cantankerous	challenge	irritation
fight	clash	abrasive
slugfest	disruption	offensive

At first glance it seems that emotional withdrawal is the opposite of the explosive argumentativeness we looked at in the last chapter. It seems that these two word lists are at opposite ends of the emotional spectrum, and in some respects they are. Yet these characteristics have more in common than is first apparent. Notice how the following words may be used to portray both withdrawal and argumentativeness:

annoyed	disturbed	stressed
upset	pained	hurt
troubled	concerned	burdened
provoked	frazzled	mad

WHAT MESSAGE LIES BENEATH WITHDRAWAL?
The single word that ties withdrawal and argumentativeness together is *fear.* That word persistently pops up when we talk about imbalanced personal traits. Surprisingly, fear lies beneath these seemingly dissimilar feelings. Notice the connection between the behaviors of these family members:

Situation: What started out as a playful argument turned into a nasty war of words as Kurtis taunted his brother, who was not as assertive as Kurtis. Walking in on the last part of their conversation, their dad quickly became enraged at Kurtis's cocky attitude, and he verbally pounced on him. Kurtis tried to defend himself by blaming his brother for what had happened. Not willing to accept any excuses from his son, the dad continued his verbal onslaught. Kurtis hung his head and endured the lecture. Later, as Kurtis sat alone in his room, he thought that maybe he would run away.

Dad's emotions: Dad's angry outburst was motivated by his fear that Kurtis would think it was acceptable to treat his brother with disrespect. He desperately wanted his boys to be friends in a way that he and his own brother had not been. He realized he was hard on his son, but he felt justified in his behavior because his concern was so strong.

Kurtis's emotions: Kurtis had not intended to get into a fight with his brother. It had just happened. Though he had not said much to his father, strong feelings surged through him. He was concerned that his dad misunderstood him, and he wanted the chance to explain himself. He did not want his dad to think so poorly of him, but it seemed that he could do nothing to erase his mistakes. He worried that he was not an important member of the family.

Analysis: The argument between Kurtis and his dad evoked fear in both of them. The father was aroused by his own haunting fears that his sons' relationship would be broken much like his relationship with his own brother had been fractured years earlier. Kurtis was afraid that his father would never understand him. A chasm stood between him and his dad. His hurt was strong enough that he felt that he might as well run away from home. Though the father and son expressed their feelings differently, both had similar root emotions.

• • • •

Situation: Barbara and James disagreed over how to handle a situation involving their daughter. Barbara had caught their child, Kristen, in a lie earlier in the day. She grounded Kristen to her room for the remainder of the day. But instead of letting her punishment stand as its own lesson, Barbara repeatedly bickered with her daughter throughout the afternoon. Her hope was to underscore the message that lying is unacceptable. When James arrived home, he was pulled into the middle of this mother-daughter dispute. He agreed with Kristen that Barbara was wrong to keep bringing up the subject of the lie. He berated his wife for her inability to drop the subject once she had taken disciplinary action. Barbara reacted to her husband by refusing to talk to him the rest of the night. Irritated by his wife's silence, James did the very thing he had chided her for doing to Kristen—he griped and fussed at her throughout the evening.

Barbara's emotions: Barbara silently protested against her husband's insensitive ways. She knew from experience that to try to explain herself to him would be useless. She wished the gnawing feeling of discomfort would go away with her silence, but it did not. Her husband's persistent remarks convinced her that she could not tell him how she really felt since his mind was bolted shut. She hated that feeling.

James's emotions: If James could name the single thing that upset him most about his family's communication, it would be that Barbara did not know when to quit harping on the children's mistakes. The last thing he wanted to see happen was a split between his wife and his children. He was so convinced that his view of the family was right that he felt compelled to press the point with Barbara. Her silence goaded him to repeat his feelings over and over again. A begging tone in his voice announced his anxiety.

Analysis: Barbara and James wanted the same thing. Each wanted the family to flow in harmony. They differed in how they handled a discipline problem with their daughter, resulting in marital friction. Barbara was afraid that her logical, insensitive husband would verbally blast her. To maintain some semblance of control over herself, she chose to keep quiet. James did all he could to engage Barbara in a dialogue. He wanted to hear her say the words, "I agree with everything you say. I was wrong to bicker with Kristen." Barbara's silence raised his anxiety level to the point that he felt out of control of his own family. Fear drove him to be contentious and argumentative, even though his actions drove a deeper wedge between himself and his wife.

WITHDRAWAL SPEAKS VOLUMES

We often think of emotional withdrawal as the absence of thoughts, feelings, or opinions about a particular matter. We assume that the withdrawn family member has little or nothing to say. But we must remember that every behavior has a purpose. Inner thoughts can be very effectively communicated through silence. Let's look at some typical messages sent through withdrawal:

- "My emotions are so strong that I might explode if I let them go."
- "I've just about given up hope that things will change for the better."
- "There's no use in talking. Others can't possibly understand me."

- "Life has been unfair to me. Why should I believe it will be different if I open up?"
- "Maybe if I hide from my feelings, they won't hurt me."
- "I feel sorry for myself and want someone to notice me."
- "No one cares about me. Why would they want to listen to my problems?"
- "I am in control of my world if I hold tightly to my inner secrets."
- "Others will think I am weak if I talk about my problems."

These are not the sentiments of an emotionally stagnant person. Can you feel the emotion's intensity, its urgency, despair, fear? Unsure that a favorable response awaits, the withdrawn family member takes what seems to be the safest route and holds tightly to his or her feelings.

Oddly enough, most withdrawn people know that something is wrong with their communication style. They recognize that they cannot express themselves the way others can, but they feel helpless to change their ways. When I've asked some withdrawn children, adolescents, and adults to talk about withdrawal, this is what they say about themselves:

- "I'm afraid I'll hurt other people's feelings if I say what I think."
- "I know I'll just get blasted if I speak up."
- "I'll be laughed at if I tell people what I think."
- "I feel so ashamed to say what I'm feeling."
- "I'm afraid people will talk about me if I tell them how I feel."

- "I'm scared to open up because then the whole world will know my business."
- "I'll just be put down again."
- "I'll be told I can't feel that way. I can't help it!"

These statements express some strong emotions. Withdrawn family members are not without feelings. The opposite is true. Through withdrawal, they are simply protecting themselves from their fears—fears of rejection, misunderstanding, further conflict, teasing, or unwanted attention. Withdrawal is a defense against these fears. It protects against things that hurt. Most withdrawn family members, especially teens and adults, will quickly say they do not like their emotional seclusion. Their hope is that family circumstances will change so they can grow into the emotionally expressive person they want to be.

JESUS AND A WITHDRAWN WOMAN
Jesus had encounters with all kinds of people, many of whom were emotionally withdrawn. One story found in John 4:1-26 goes into considerable detail to portray a conversation between Jesus and an unnamed woman. She may have been a recluse; she chose to go to the well at a time when the other women in the town would not be there. She was an object of gossip, and she knew it. She was a failure in marital relationships and had already had five husbands. To her, it was simply best to keep out of harm's way.

Scripture records at least part of the conversation between Jesus and this woman. We are told that Jesus offered her hope for a more meaningful life than what she was experiencing. What we are not told is the manner in which Jesus spoke to this person. My hunch is that through his sympathetic ways he convinced her that he accepted her. His facial expression was no doubt kind. His tone of voice suggested it was safe to confide in him, which I would imagine the woman did. He avoided comments that would make her feel uncomfortable. Although Jesus did not condone her lifestyle, it was evident to her that he did not judge her. Her response was an enthusiastic acceptance of his assertion that he could show her a better way of living.

Too often when we encounter people who are like this withdrawn, unnamed woman, we react in ways that drive them into more intense isolation. When this person is a family member, emotional pain enters the home and grips the family unit. We often make false assumptions about withdrawn people.

- They choose to be the way they are, so they do not deserve our sympathy.
- They don't want to be close to others, so we will let them be isolated.
- They like being the way they are, so there is no use trying to change them.
- They don't listen to our good advice, so we will not give it.
- They are intellectually slow, so they need our constant attention and direction.
- They were born that way, so we cannot change them.

The unnamed woman described in John's Gospel was like most withdrawn people. She wanted to be honest with herself and others, but she could not unless she was convinced that she was safe. Jesus offered her that release, and she accepted it. As family leaders, you can invite the same reaction from withdrawn family members when you follow these guidelines:

- Separate your disagreement of their actions from your judgment of them.
- Communicate understanding of their viewpoint, even though you see things differently.
- Wait until the time is right to offer your opinion, if you offer it at all.
- Use physical touch as a way of communicating emotional acceptance.
- Say aloud what you think they feel as a way of showing your understanding.
- Allow them to disagree with you, knowing that their position may not be permanent.
- Refuse to force your feelings and opinions onto others.
- Be consistently kind as a way of proving your trustworthiness.

CASE STUDY: MARK REVEALS THE REASON BEHIND HIS BEHAVIOR

One of the most delightful boys I have counseled was a withdrawn boy whose sensitive nature led him to keep his feelings to himself rather than risk being hurt by his gruff family. To say that he was different from his parents and older sister was an understatement. The other three people in his home were strong willed and assertive. Where Mark had problems saying what he felt, the rest of the family had no problem—none at all.

After Mark and I became good friends, I suggested that we meet together with the rest of his family so we could share some of our insights with his parents and sister. At first he was mortified, but when I assured him I would be his ally, he consented. Once the family was seated in my office, I explained what I hoped to achieve during our conference.

"Mark and I have had some good discussions about his feelings about himself. He knows that the rest of you are worried about him because he seems so unhappy. We agreed that it would be helpful for the three of you to understand how he feels. I'd like to guide Mark through some of his thoughts with the hope that we can figure out some ways to make it easier for him to be more at ease. Mark and I will talk to each other while you observe."

I then turned my face and attention to Mark. "Mark, I would like us to start by talking about the loneliness you've felt. You've told me that one of the things that hurts most is that no one sees the things you see at home."

"That's about it. You just said it. Nobody understands me, so there's no use in trying to talk to them."

"Your family is concerned that you're withdrawn. They fear that they're going to lose touch with you."

"Probably."

"You mean there's a good chance that you could break away from the family?"

"I already have."

"Oh? How's that?"

"They do their thing, and I do my thing. It's that simple."

"And that must be where the loneliness comes in. You're isolated in your own home."

"Yeah. I guess I am. But that's kind of good."

"Good?"

"Yeah. I mean, I hate being to myself, but I don't get mad about the things they do. I just don't care."

"So being withdrawn is a sad and lonely feeling in one sense, but it keeps you out of fights and arguments."

"Yeah, but . . ." Mark's voice trailed off as a distant look crossed his eyes.

"Go ahead."

"I don't know. I can't. They'd get mad."

"Who would get mad?"

"Them," he said, nodding to his parents and sister.

"They're just observing. You and I are the ones having the conversation."

Mark nodded his head, indicating that he didn't mind telling me his thoughts. "I think about running away all the time. It's just that I don't know where I'd go. If I had some place to run to, I'd probably be there already."

"If you say those kinds of things out loud, you're afraid that someone's going to pounce on you and tell you to snap out of it, to quit thinking the way you do."

"Do you know how many times I've heard that? A lot. People tell me all the time that I should quit being the way I am. How can I?"

"You mean you'd like to do things differently, but you don't know how?"

"Sure, I'd like to be a part of the family. Sometimes I try, but when I do, they criticize me because I'm not like them. They're loud, and they fight and slug it out. I'm not that way."

"So it would be easier just to leave."

"Not really. I mean, then who would I have to turn to?"

"Are you saying you'd like to turn to your family, but you can't?"

"Yeah. I'd like to . . . I try to, but . . ." Mark shook his head again and quit talking. A moment passed.

"Mark, your family thinks you don't care. You do though, don't you?"

"A lot."

"When you keep your feelings to yourself, you probably secretly hope that someone in your family will tell you they understand how isolated you feel. You keep hoping."

Mark lifted his eyebrows as he looked me in the eye. Though he did not say anything, his gesture suggested that he wanted more than anything to be given the hope that he could emotionally reunite with the family. As we sat there in my office, I quickly glanced at Mark's sister and parents. They had paid close attention to every word and gesture Mark had made. Though Mark did not realize it at the time, he had gotten through to them.

• • • •

At the outset of this chapter I noted that withdrawal and argumentativeness seem to be opposite emotional expressions. Yet fear pulls these two extreme expressions close together. In the same way that argumentative people take a risk that they can forcefully blast their feelings into the open, withdrawn people hope that someone will take the risk of entering their world with comprehension and acceptance.

If one or more of your family members withdraw,

you can help them open up by helping them feel safe. Resist the need to judge or correct. Look beneath the behavior to the underlying message of fear. Then do what you can to lessen those fears.

Summary: When people withdraw, we should not assume that they have nothing to say or that they have no feelings. For them, withdrawal may be the safest way to deal with emotions. Most withdrawn people want others to draw them out, but they will allow themselves to open up only if we show patient understanding. Providing a safe environment for them to express themselves will help alleviate the fear that underlies their withdrawal.

1. When you communicate with a withdrawn family member, use these guidelines to draw that person out of his or her shell.

- Try to put yourself in the shoes of that person. Think the way he or she thinks, even if it varies widely from your own way of thinking.
- Say out loud what you think that person may be thinking or feeling. If you are wrong, the person will correct you. If you are accurate, that person may elaborate further.
- Anytime the withdrawn person offers an opinion or comment, ask for further details. You probably are seeing only the tip of the emotional iceberg.
- Let time be a healing agent. Refrain from offering quick solutions to problems that took a long time to create. The first need of the withdrawn person is to feel accepted.

2. We have seen that withdrawn family members often have difficulty saying what they feel. You can help them by putting labels on their emotions. Not only will you help your family members understand themselves, but you will also open the door for productive family dialogues. Practice using sentences that start with the following phrases:

- "You usually . . ."
- "You must have felt . . ."
- "And that left you thinking . . ."
- "I'll bet you . . ."
- "You've got to wonder . . ."
- "You probably . . ."
- "I can only imagine you felt . . ."
- "Sometimes it seems . . ."
- "When that happens you . . ."
- "It's no wonder you . . ."
- "It embarrassed you to . . ."
- "All you wanted was . . ."

3. In trying to reach family members who have withdrawn from you, try some of the following activities as a means of reestablishing an emotional connection between the two of you:

- Spend at least fifteen minutes doing something together. Let it be something the other family member wants to do, whether it is to play a board game, lie on the bed and talk about nothing in particular, play catch with a ball in the yard, or bake something. Refrain from heavy conversation. Make it your goal simply to have a pleasant time together.
- Write a note letting that family member know that he or she means a lot to you. Go ahead and be mushy. Follow up with a hug.
- Think of a rift that has come between the two of you. Even if it was not your fault, do whatever is necessary to remove the barrier that separates you. You will be sending a potent message that

you are more concerned about being in a right relationship with that family member than just being right.

CHAPTER EIGHT

Indulgence: Taking All That Life Offers

OUR family is fortunate to have experienced friendships with people from different cultures. Living in a university town, we have been hosts to numerous international students who have come to our city for special studies. Most summers our family becomes the surrogate parents and siblings of Japanese university students on an exchange tour of the United States. As a part of their educational experience, the students live several days with an American family to experience real "Yankee" life. Of course, my wife, children, and I benefit from their visits every bit as much as they do.

Invariably, these students are struck by the brazen lifestyle we Americans live. They comment on how open we are compared with their own families. They notice how materialistic most Americans are—even those who seemingly do not have lots of money. The international students are overwhelmed by our emphasis on winning. They are frightened at the lengths to which Americans will go to impose their will on others. They are dumbfounded at the crime rate and can find no logical explanation for why we so willingly rob, hurt, humiliate, and even annihilate one another. Hardly a summer visit passes without a discussion of how Americans are such self-centered people.

I have yet to find good answers to these students' questions. Excuses and rationalizations are easy to come by, but answers evade me.

Sobered by the observations of these foreign friends, I have begun to notice how indulgence pervades our homes. Even when we try to teach humility and sacrifice, the subtle messages of a pleasure-seeking, power-mongering, competition-driven world invade our family structure. Notice how indulgence can weave its way into the home, as the following three scenarios illustrate.

Franklin was mad. It seemed he was annoyed most of his waking moments. He believed his family enjoyed torturing him. Earlier that day his mother had forced him to do thirty minutes of yard work before he could play with the kids down the street. His younger brother had slipped into his room that morning and had "borrowed" his watch. Franklin was incensed to find an ugly scratch on its face. He felt completely justified in hitting his brother. He wanted everyone to know that he was in charge of his life and his possessions. After his mother spanked him, Franklin sat in his room nursing his sore backside and equally wounded ego. He haughtily announced to anyone who would listen, "I'm not through showing you that I won't be treated like this. Nobody can make me do what I don't want to do!"

• • • •

Cal sat at his desk and worked on a project his boss
wanted completed yesterday. He hardly noticed when
a coworker slipped in holding a large brown envelope
in his hand. "You got a minute, Cal? It's that time of
the year." Cal looked up, perturbed that he was being
disturbed. He had important work to do. His uninvited
guest continued, "We hope to have 100 percent partici-
pation in this year's Christmas fund drive. So far, everyone I've asked has contributed. How about you? What
can I put you down for?"

Cal did not try to hide his disgust. "A buck," he
muttered. "I'll give it to you later." He then buried his
head in his work, silently signaling it was time for the
coworker to shove off. Cal later griped to himself that
he wished people would quit hounding him for charitable contributions. He felt he should be free to decide
who would receive his donations. The thing was,
though, that Cal's sole charitable gift of the year was
that forced contribution of one dollar. He felt that he
deserved every penny he earned.

• • • •

Kelli sat in the school counselor's office, trying to
explain her recent behavior. She had been caught
cheating on a test. Rather than punish her, the teacher
thought it wiser to see that the girl get help for her
problems. Not only did Kelli cheat whenever she got
the chance, she refused to follow even the simplest of
classroom instructions. None of the students associated
with her, except the ones who showed a similar bad
attitude. Explaining herself to the counselor, Kelli

angrily said, "You can call my mother and tell her what I've done, but I'll guarantee you she won't care. She'll say she does, but if she cares so much about me, tell me why she never even talks to me except to yell? And my stepdad will just hit me if he finds out. He thinks that's the answer to everything. You've got to beat the meanness out of people like me. Ask him, that's what he'll tell you! I've learned that if I'm going to make it in this world, I've got to put *me* first."

HOW INDULGENCE PROMOTES A
SELF-CENTERED LIFESTYLE

We live in a society that makes it easy for us to indulge ourselves. In various ways we are told that we deserve special treatment. We are encouraged to toss guilt aside in favor of self-gratification. If something feels good, society says, "Just do it!" Whatever our impulse, we are urged to act on it. Play now and pay later. On and on the messages go, telling the world that an indulged life is the good life.

Families respond differently to this pressure. Some become permissive or indulge themselves and their children. Others rigidly try to fight the pressures of the world. Others hopelessly withdraw from the world, thinking they cannot keep up with all its pressures. Given the indulgent messages of our culture, consider the following questions:

- How do these messages affect the lifestyle of the typical American family?
- How do these messages affect your family?
- Do most families avoid the pressures of the

world, give into them, or ignore them? Why do
you think this is so?

- How does your family handle these pressures?

There is nothing wrong with looking out for personal
needs. We have already seen that it is important to take
care of ourselves so that we can in turn give abundantly
to others. Yet families may find themselves in an iron-
clad struggle against self-centeredness. Jesus recognized
this ceaseless conflict and spoke at length about it in
the Sermon on the Mount (Matthew 6:19-34). God
does not want us to ignore our personal needs, but he
does want us to live a lifestyle that includes sharing
ourselves with others.

Several behavioral patterns reflect that family members value themselves at the expense of others: indiffer-
ence, pride, arrogance, entitlement, temper tantrums,
and emptiness. The presence of any of these characteristics may be a red flag that indulgence and self-
centeredness are in the home. Listen to what family
members have said to me about these behavior patterns.

Indifference

Child: Why do I always have to do what you ask
me to do? Why do I have to help? I don't care if
you think it's good for me. I'm not interested.

Father: I know it hurts his feelings when I talk to
him like that. Why do you think I'm hard on the
boy? He needs to be hurt. If he doesn't know what
it's like to be low man on the totem pole, he'll
never have any respect for others.

Pride

> **Sister:** I'm glad my brother did a good job in his game, but if I tell him he did, he'll just get the big head. I don't know why, but I just can't say things like that to him. Maybe I'm rude, but that's the way it is.

> **Parent:** I probably shouldn't have said that to my child, but if you ask me, he had it coming to him. When he's willing to admit to his mistakes, then maybe I'll admit mine.

Arrogance

> **Teenager:** Sure, I'm trouble for my parents. They think they can tell me how to think, how to act, and who to hang out with. I'm not saying my parents are stupid, but I think I know more about what I need than they do. I'm a lot smarter than they think I am. I know what I need, and I'm not about to let my parents push me around.

> **Father:** I'm pretty sick of hearing these counselors tell me I need to be more loving. How do they know what goes on in this family? Let them live a day in this house, and they'll see why I'm the way I am. I can't stand it when people talk down to me.

Entitlement

> **Six-year-old:** I don't want to wait. You told me I could have it, and I want it now! You're not being fair!

Mother: I don't think I should have to beg my children for respect. I'm their mother and should be treated with respect for no other reason than that.

Temper Tantrums

Parent: That's the last time you'll talk to me like that! If you think I'm going to take your defiance sitting down, you've got another think coming to you. Rude children like you deserve to sit in their room until they rot. And if you *do* rot, don't blame me. I'm not the one filling your head with all that putrid filth!

Child: I hate you! I hate everyone in this house! I'm not going to do what you tell me. I'm not! An army can't make me!

Emptiness

Husband: Sometimes I wonder if anyone even knows I exist. I even wonder what my family thinks about me. My wife does her thing without even consulting with me, and my kids act as if I'm an embarrassment to the world. It makes me want to chuck it all and live life the way I want to. What difference would it make anyway? I honestly doubt that anyone would notice.

Preadolescent: I don't even know what you're talking about when you ask about my family. What family? My mother can't decide who she wants to marry, so she goes from one man to another. And the men she chooses treat me like dirt. My brother's not any better. He beats on me whenever he feels like it. Family? I don't have one. All I've got is me.

WHAT MESSAGE LIES BENEATH INDULGENT BEHAVIOR?
Indulgent family members send a common message, one that may be surprising. These people desire to find meaning in life, even though they attempt it through skewed behavior. Living an indulged lifestyle encourages risk taking. The risk comes in the vain hope that they will find happiness in personal pleasure without having to share with others. Although our society encourages the family to be self-indulgent, it gives no guarantees that an indulgent lifestyle will lead to personal satisfaction. I find that self-absorbed people have deeper needs that beg to be voiced. Listen to some of the thoughts voiced by these family members:

The indifferent child: If I try to get involved with my family, maybe they'll reject me. It could happen, you know. At times I feel left out. It's easier just to do my own thing. Sure, I hear what my parents are saying, but I tune them out. That way I can dump them before they dump me.

The arrogant parent: Okay, so I say things I shouldn't to my family. But do you know how much respect I get when I say what I really feel? None! I want to feel important. That's why I come on so strong!

The cocky teenager: I've tried the nice-guy routine, and it got me nowhere. If you don't come right out and say what you think, you're going to get run over. At least I do in my family. I wish it weren't that way, but it is.

The self-centered mother: I don't want to be ignored. It makes me feel like a nobody. That's how I felt when I was a kid—as if nobody cared about me. I just want my day in the sun. I refuse to let my husband and kids treat me the way I was treated as a child. It's not wrong to do that, is it?

The child who throws tantrums: I never know when people are listening and when they're putting me off. The worst feeling in the world is when nobody will listen to me. I show my feelings so that my family will have to notice me. But they *still* don't get my message!

The empty father: Life's a bore. I've got nothing to gain when I try to tell my family what I think. They don't understand. I've learned to deal with the pain. Might as well, because it's not going away.

Underlying the words of these family members runs a common thread: dissatisfaction. We don't normally think of the indulgent person as depressed, but that's exactly what many people report when they dare talk about themselves honestly. It's strange that an indulged lifestyle convinces people to dress up their feelings with pride or arrogance or through tantrums or emptiness or any other kind of dressing, but it does. And just as indulgence covers true feelings, it also hides real communication. When stripped to the emotional bone, self-centered people tell surprising tales of pain.

Content people find it unnecessary to focus so heavily on their own personal needs. After all, those needs have been adequately met. When indulgence shows up in families, messages of unhappiness are usually bubbling just beneath family members' words and behavior.

INDULGENCE EXPRESSES ITSELF IN PERMISSIVENESS

I once sat with a group of teenagers who were free to talk about any topic that related to the family. They held nothing back. At first they talked about their siblings and then their parents. They were blunt in their comments—boy, were they ever! Eventually the discussion got around to rules. I suppose the transition from siblings to parents to rules was predictable. After all, when young people think of parents, one of the first things that comes to mind is that parents are the rule makers in their life.

The topic turned to the issue of curfews. Most of the teens had one. Few of them liked it. They complained that their parents didn't trust them. They claimed they could monitor their behavior without a curfew. They railed on the bad teenagers whose behavior caused all other parents to impose restrictions on them. Of course, the kids in the group did not consider themselves to be one of the "bad" teens that compelled adults to be strict.

I was reminded of that particular conversation several weeks later when I met with a group of parents. These adults, just like the teenagers, were free to talk about any topic that dealt with family relations. They wound their way from one issue to another before settling on their obligation to impose limits on thoughtless, impulsive children. One father spoke up, "I don't like to restrict my kids, but I have to. My son forced me to put a curfew on him because he wouldn't come home unless he was told he *had* to be in at a certain time. And he's only twelve years old!"

"That's nothing," said another dad. "My son is just seven, and we have to put limits on his playtime. If we don't, he'll stay outside all night, playing or riding his bike. He has no concept of time."

When I asked the parents if they enjoyed restricting their children, nearly all of them claimed that they did not. One mother said, "It would be perfectly fine with me if my children could make their own rules. If I knew they would stick by them, I'd let them."

Paralleling their children's feelings, parents agree that they are tougher on their kids than they want to be. They believe that if other parents were more responsible, they could be more permissive with their children. And just like the kids, few parents consider themselves to be "bad" parents.

Children and teenagers like to live with relatively few rules. Likewise, parents would prefer to avoid having to dictate rules. Put another way, both kids and parents would like to live in a permissive world. Understanding that dynamic of human behavior helps to explain why our society has become so indulgent. It's what we all want.

Permissiveness shows up in families in varied ways. Listen to the comments made by family members on this issue.

> ***Mother:*** I told Naomi she couldn't have this expensive purse she's been begging me for. I think I convinced her that she wasn't going to get it, but

on her birthday I surprised her with it. You'd better believe she was excited.

Friend: Seeing her so excited probably did you as much good as it did Naomi.

Mother: It did. I felt like a kid again. I figured she would appreciate the surprise.

Friend: Did she?

Mother: At first she did, but now she wants a leather coat even worse than she wanted the purse.

••••

First father: I told Antonio he couldn't play baseball this year. Last year when he played, he didn't get along at all with the coach. He cried after every practice because the coach pushed him so hard. When I found out that the same man would be his coach this year, I put my foot down. Antonio begged me to let him join something. I didn't really want to since he can't handle the stress.

Second father: I doubt that Antonio understood your decision.

First father: He didn't. I made up for it by buying a membership in a health club. I think Antonio will like it. It will help take his mind off not playing baseball this year. He wants to take racquetball lessons. They're expensive, but if it will help him out, then it's worth it.

• • • •

Wife: Every time I tell the kids they can't do something, you go behind my back to make sure that they get what they want. It's as if my word holds no weight in the home.

Husband: I think you're too strict. I don't think it hurts the kids to be given a little freedom. I'm not trying to undermine your authority. I'm simply trying to help them out.

Wife: Don't you think I want what's best for the kids too? You're such a pushover that the kids have no respect for you. At the same time, you're making them hate me!

• • • •

Father: Sure, the kids get into trouble. That's a part of growing up. They don't do anything I didn't do when I was growing up.

School counselor: Even so, I suspect it gets under your skin when the school calls to tell you how your children have misbehaved again.

Father: Sometimes. But to tell you the truth, I don't get too upset. I mean, they're just children. They'll grow out of it. I did.

••••

Permissiveness shows up in a variety of family behaviors, like those seen above. Permissiveness indulges children, giving them more than they need. It involves

- making excuses for children's behavior
- looking the other way when children blunder
- finding someone or something else to blame
- putting off consequences that could prevent future problems
- assuming that children will learn from their experiences
- refusing to live emotionally separated from the children
- allowing children to make decisions that fail to match their maturity level
- consistently giving in to children's pleas
- searching to fix problems the child should independently resolve

Not only can parents be permissive in dealing with children, they may also be permissive with *themselves*. Adults who place loose boundaries on their own behavior can send the wrong message to their children. Parents can be permissive with themselves by

- setting rules that they themselves are not willing to keep
- spending time pursuing personal gain rather than family goals
- putting off until tomorrow what should be done today

- allowing laziness to overcome personal discipline
- indulging in material gain over family need
- turning over the task of nurturing the children to others
- claiming adult privilege as an excuse for excessive behavior
- living for today with a limited view for the future

As you study patterns that affect home life, look not only at the children's behavior but also at the adults' behavior. A child's behavior does not exist in a vacuum. It is sculpted by relationships, communication, and the role models who illustrate how life is to be lived. One of the more frightening realities of family life is that parents are always on stage.

Like children's behavior, parents' behavior is also shaped by time and experience. The makeup of the family constellation, the adult's own past, the children's personalities, and the success or failure of relationships influence adult behavior. This combination of factors blends together to create a unique set of dynamics.

DEFEAT INDULGENCE BY BALANCING SELF WITH OTHERS
Quite obviously, the opposite of an indulgent lifestyle is one centered on others. Jesus teaches what the essence of that lifestyle is in his Sermon on the Mount (Matthew 5–7). He teaches that we should get rid of any habits or actions that would cause us to fall into sin. We should be people of integrity, keeping our promises to others. Our speech should be plain and truthful. When other people harm us, we should deny the urge to retaliate and instead should seek to do good to the person who harmed us. We should love

our enemies and the unlovable. When we do charitable things, we should do them without fanfare. Our prayers are to be a humble acknowledgment of our need for God's strength.

As we direct our families toward an others-centered lifestyle, we can learn from Christ's teachings. These four principles guide family growth.

Establish family guidelines and stick to them. Teach by example that rules are meant not only for others but also for you. Remember, our children are more affected by our behavior than by our words. Live according to what you believe. If our children hear us saying to a friend that we value family time, then we must make sure we live out that belief. Avoid making frequent exceptions to the rules, both for your children and for yourself. Reward behaviors that pull the family together rather than tear it apart. Be sympathetic when your children disagree with you, but stick to your principles. Be willing to set aside momentary pleasure for future, more lasting gratification.

Avoid family communication traps. Recognize one another's sensitive traits. Avoid pouncing on those weak spots. Let the past be just that. Refuse to resurrect dead issues. Stay away from negative predictions about one another—they just may come true. Wait until the right time to criticize. If you learn to listen and express understanding, you may not need to criticize at all. Affirm your children and your spouse whenever you can.

Teach the need to be responsible to others. Balance giving to self with giving to others. Shower praise on children, especially young ones, for being considerate to others. Take turns going first and being last. Determine who will be responsible for specific chores. Help one another out. Show flexibility in making choices. Be democratic in your leadership.

Keep family life from becoming skewed in the wrong direction. Hold family talks about matters of social and moral significance. Provide for your family's material needs, but not to excess. Consider each family member's needs as you make decisions. Love each other openly. Plan recreational activities that involve the entire family. Listen to each other's thoughts and feelings without needing to correct. Become involved in each other's special interests. Respect differences of opinions. Refuse to force your will on others.

ERASE INDULGENCE BY FACING LIFE'S STRUGGLES

Many of us have bought into the cultural lie that the good life is an easy life. And in trying to make their lives easier, many parents indulge themselves and their children. It is not particularly wrong to want a life free from trial. But to set out to find an easy way to family living almost always results in disappointment, if not utter defeat.

Scripture counters that cultural lie by reminding us that the good life is one lived in obedience to God, and that may involve hardship and struggle. Most of us try to avoid tough situations at all cost. Others of us bail out of life itself whenever a trial appears. The thing is, we cannot avoid struggles. They are inevitable.

The Old Testament character Jacob struggled with life. The Bible records one particular emotional tussle that lasted all night. We know that up to this point in his life, Jacob had tried to live the easy life. He had deceived his father and estranged himself from his amily in the process. When he struggled with God that night, he emerged a changed man. The struggle made Jacob a stronger man. The conflict was good for him. He grew from it.

Of course, I do not advocate that family members intentionally brawl with one another for the sake of creating healthy conflict. And we don't need to hunt for struggles outside the home. Conflict will find us no matter how hard we try to hide from it. When inevitable difficulties strike, family members need skills to meet life's challenges head-on. The easy life is not necessarily good for a family. In fact, trials can strengthen families.

Listen to the comments made by family members who have weathered some of life's worst storms:

> *A mother whose first child died at birth:* At the time, I thought I would die too. I felt so overwhelmingly helpless. But now we have two girls, and I've never felt so much love from any two individuals. I think the tragedy of losing our first child helped me learn how to love.

> *A businessman who nearly died in an automobile accident:* Before my accident, about the only thing I was concerned with was making enough money to retire at an early age. I still think that would be nice, but I can tell you that I'm much more concerned about living a full life before I retire.

> *Teenager who survived a suicide attempt:* I used to think I had no friends. I was ashamed of what I

did, but my friends told me that didn't matter to
them. Maybe I have more friends than I thought.

Wife whose vehicle was stolen: I was scared to death
when I came out and saw that my car was gone.
My first thought was, *What if the kids and I had
been in it when the thief came?* Somehow, I didn't
care about the car because I knew we were safe.

••••

If you or your spouse or children have become indulgent, you can break the pattern. Allow God to show
you your self-centeredness, and ask him to show you
how to respond to other family members' indulgent
behavior. Don't run from the difficulties of life. Trust
that they can be effective tools to help you and your
family grow. Use the hard times to teach valuable
lessons that can result in positive change.

Summary: The indulgence that pervades our society
also infiltrates our homes, often appearing as permissiveness. In our quest for the good life, we often take
the easy way out, saying yes to ourselves and our children when we should be saying no. As we recognize
indulgence in our families, we can work to bring
balance to our lives.

Part 2 has helped us look at how we can handle five
destructive behavior patterns: rigidity, dependence,
argumentativeness, withdrawal, and indulgence. Part 3
will look at two key questions that influence our families: Who's in control? and How do we build self-
esteem?

FAMILY NOTES

1. Evaluate yourself and your family members. Where do you see indulgent behavior infiltrating your family life? What will you do about it?

2. How strict should you be in discouraging an imbalanced lifestyle for your children?

3. What should you do when your children demand the easy life?

4. Select from among the following activities designed to move the family away from self-centeredness to a more balanced lifestyle. Some of these ventures may be difficult to do, but try them.

- Take an inventory of how much time your family spends in front of the television set. Determine that for one week each family member will cut his or her viewing time in half. At the end of that week discuss the effects of your experiment on family life.
- Calculate how much money your family spends on frivolous items or activities. (You decide how you will define "frivolous.") Cut that amount of spending in half for at least one week. Again, meet as a family to discuss the effects of your temporary change in spending habits.

- Instead of giving a material gift to a family member, give a gift of service. You might do that person's chores or fulfill a task that he or she wants to see done. Give your gift with enthusiasm.

5. In my counseling practice, I keep notes on the families with whom I work. I often write down significant statements family members make. Not only does this exercise help me understand the family's mind-set, but it also provides useful anecdotal information about family life in general. The following are comments some of my child clients have made about permissiveness. By examining these comments, we can better understand the reasons kids act as they do. In turn, we can be better prepared to respond to real family needs.

- "I don't pay any attention to my mother's threats. She always backs down. You know, she hates to punish me."
- "I know how to get my dad to give in. I bring up something that he's done wrong. It shuts him up real fast. Then I get my way!"
- "My parents don't care about me. They let me do anything I want."
- "My teacher said she was calling my mother. So what! I can make my mother believe me. It works every time."
- "The only family I've got is myself. In our house, we all do our own thing. We're not a family. We just live together."
- "My parents don't know what I'm doing when I'm out. They never ask any questions. What am I supposed to do, tell them what I'm into? No

way. On second thought, I don't care if they
know; they wouldn't do anything about it."

6. I find it valuable to try to think the way another
person thinks. If I can achieve that goal, I find myself
less judgmental and more understanding of that person's behavior. Hence, I study comments like those
above to learn to think the way families think. We have
to remember that thinking as others think is not the
same as agreeing with them. A family leader can fully
understand another family member and yet completely
disagree with him or her. Family members respond
positively to people who understand their problems.
As family leaders, we can greatly increase our influence
over our children if we commit to listening and understanding the message behind their indulgent behavior.

7. Read John 3:1-21 for an example of how Jesus
responded to Nicodemus, who asked what he must do
to achieve eternal life. Keep in mind that Nicodemus
was a Pharisee, part of an imbalanced group of religious
leaders who displayed an odd blend of rigidity, withdrawal, argumentativeness, and even certain indul-
gences.

8. Read Ecclesiastes 5:10 with your family and discuss
the place money should have in your family.

9. Read Mark 8:34-36 with your family and discuss
what it means to deny ourselves and follow Christ.
Share stories of people who have found a rich, meaningful life by giving it away to Jesus.

10. Read 1 Timothy 6:6-11 with your family and discuss what it means to be contented. List ways in which your family can pursue "righteousness, godliness, faith, love, endurance and gentleness" rather than what our society claims to be the good life.

Respond Rather Than React

CHAPTER NINE

Who's in Control of the Family?

J ESSE knew he was treading on thin ice. He was just about as big as his brother, Todd, and had developed the habit of slipping into his brother's closet to pick out a shirt or pants to wear. At first, Todd tolerated his younger brother's actions. He figured it wouldn't do much harm to let Jesse occasionally use his things, as long as he showed proper care.

The trouble was, Jesse had no more concern for Todd's belongings than he did his own. That is a subtle way of saying that he was plenty rough on his brother's clothing. He not only soiled one of Todd's favorite shirts, he gave it a permanent stain. The knees of Todd's best jeans were worn thin in only one day by the younger sibling. The elder child's understandable complaints reached such a crescendo that the boys' parents made a rule that each child was to wear his own clothes and no one else's.

Jesse could not have cared less about his parents' rule. If he felt like wearing Todd's clothes, he intended to do just that, despite what he had been told. On this particular day, he chose to wear his brother's multicolored plaid shirt to school. It was as if he purposely selected the loudest shirt in Todd's closet as a way of announcing, "I know what the rules are around here, and I don't intend to keep them!"

As Jesse walked into the kitchen, he casually asked, "What's for breakfast?"

"Same as usual—cereal and toast. You want yours buttered before or after I stick it in the toaster oven?"

Jesse's mother had spoken without looking up at her child. Whirling around to put something in the refrigerator, she immediately noticed that the younger child was wearing Todd's shirt. Her heart sank as she thought to herself, *Oh no. Not that. I don't want to go through a fight this morning. Please, Jesse. Tell me you didn't do it.* She looked at the boy again and recognized that smug expression that always spelled trouble. She thought, *I am not going to get into a fight with that boy. I'll just let his dad handle it when he sees the shirt on Jesse.*

Just moments later Jesse's dad entered the kitchen. His head stuck in the morning newspaper, he mumbled, "Good morning," and made his way to his usual spot at the table. About to greet Jesse, he looked up, and before he could ask, "How did you sleep last night?" his eyes were pulled to the rainbow of colors on the shirt Jesse wore. Dropping the paper to the table, he did not attempt to hide his emotions as he accused his son. "Jesse, I've told you I don't know how many times *not* to wear your brother's clothes. You know the rules. Now get back to your room and take that thing off! I'm not going to watch you and Todd fight anymore about who's wearing what."

Jesse was motionless. He simply sat in his chair like a lump. He had decided that this was the shirt he wanted to wear to school that day, and he felt no compulsion to ask anyone's opinion. He did not want to give in.

"Well, did you hear me?"

A slight grunt was followed by Jesse's low voice. "Todd said I could."

Jesse's dad knew he was being duped. Calling his elder son as a lawyer would call a witness to the stand, he hollered, "Todd?"

"Sir?" came the reply from the other end of the house.

"Did you know Jesse is wearing your shirt—the plaid one with all the colors?"

"He'd better not be!"

Armed with all the evidence he needed to pronounce a verdict, Jesse's father fixed his stare back on Jesse and said, "Take the shirt off! Now! I'm sick and tired of the way you disregard the rules around here. And I don't like the way you lie about things either. Either take the shirt off, or I'll take it off for you."

Jesse's mom watched the drama from her spot only a few feet from the kitchen table. She had witnessed this scene far more times than she would have liked, and often she too had been a part of its unfolding. She felt a tinge of guilt that she had dumped this problem on her husband, but she simply did not want a headache so early in the day. Her stomach jerked as she heard Jesse defend himself, saying, "Mom didn't say anything about it when I came in. Why should you?"

"I don't care what your mother said. She may be

afraid of you, but I'm not. You're not leaving this house today with that shirt on."

That was it. Jesse's mom could not allow that curt comment to whiz right by her without reacting. "I beg your pardon! I noticed the shirt the same as you did. I had no intentions of letting him wear it. Am I guilty just because I wanted a few minutes of peace before I had to say something to that inconsiderate boy?"

"Inconsiderate? How can I be inconsiderate when all I did was put on a shirt? Give me a break!" Shoving his chair to the wall, Jesse stood up and stomped out of the room. When he returned, he had changed shirts but wore the same disposition. Little was said the rest of the morning as the family mechanically readied itself for the day.

WHO'S IN CHARGE HERE?

Control. We all want it, and sometimes we will do anything to maintain it.

The problem is, everyone else in the family wants it too. No matter how healthy a family is, the control issue will force itself to the forefront of the family agenda. No question about it. At all ages, family members want a voice in what happens to them. From the tiniest infant to the elderly grandparent, everyone wants to feel in control of his or her corner of the world.

I do. And so do you.

When we are in control, we feel important. We may even feel an addicting surge of power when we realize that our behavior has an effect on others. That feeling is reinforcing. Once we experience it, we want to feel it again.

The struggle for control in families begins as soon as the family unit is melded. Presumably, a newly married couple feels secure in knowing that they can rely on each other to fulfill their basic need for security. Yet life's trials can introduce conflicts that cause this secure feeling to erode. Arguments become more frequent. Communication is less than honest. The husband and wife play marital tug-of-war as they scurry to keep from losing control.

Then children come along. From the time they are born, children make unreasonable demands. Babies cry to be fed every hour on the hour. They arch their backs when they want to stay up and play rather than lie quietly in their cribs. As they grow older, they explore every nook and cranny in their worlds, discovering what they can dominate and what will dominate them. As children acquire language, they learn that words are magical. Used creatively, words can melt the hardest adults into soft butter. Words can also be weapons to ward off unwanted things such as chores, homework, piano practice, good manners, or consideration for others.

Through this struggle, children are seeking security. They want to have a voice in the way their world is run. It occurs at all age levels and in each stage of life. The struggle for control may be a vicious fight or a passive refusal to let go of what feels safe.

Notice the elements of control in the following behavior patterns of family members:

- A mother reasons with her daughter to study harder in school. She hopes to convince her that she can be anything she wants to be. She wants so much to see her daughter succeed that she practically does the girl's work for her.

- A husband runs the family with an iron fist. He holds an important position in the community and does not want to show any public evidence of personal weakness. He explodes when he hears that a family member has gotten out of line.

- A normally compliant boy shuts down when his teacher asks him to explain why he did not complete his homework. She only wants to make sure he understood the assignment, but he thinks she wants to humiliate him in front of his friends.

- A brother warns his sister that if she wants to avoid his wrath, she will keep her mouth shut when her parents ask questions about his "partying." He firmly informs her that what he does with his friends is his business and no one else's.

- A toddler looks his mother straight in the eye as he reaches in a box to retrieve a favored toy she had repossessed only moments earlier. When he is told no, he defies his mother's warning, silently challenging her to an emotional sparring match.

The struggle for control in the family follows a predictable course. First, a family member presents a problem, whether it is an intentional violation of rules, a stubborn refusal to give in, or an unwillingness to cooperate. Second, another family member tries to force a solution that is different from the solution the first family member wants. The first family member searches for a way to salvage a victory in this struggle. The struggle for control shifts from a *contest for behavioral control* to a *battle of emotional willpower.*

Note how a family member may lose the struggle for behavioral control yet win the power struggle:

- A boy may grudgingly agree to take out the kitchen trash, but he delights in knowing that he has created a foul mood that smells as bad as his attitude.
- A child may complete her homework at her mother's urging, but she learns that when she complains that her work is too hard, her mother will come to her rescue.
- Kids may comply with their father's strict rules, but they are convinced that he cannot possibly understand their feelings.
- A toddler does not get to play with the toy his mother made him put away, but he recognizes that her patience is running thin. He correctly surmises that she will not last long before giving in to his demands.

HAVE YOU LOST CONTROL?

Take this simple test to see if you feel out of control in any aspect of your family life. Answer yes or no to each of the following statements:

Yes   No   "My child's behavior is completely out of bounds."

Yes   No   "I feel helpless to make my kids get along with each other."

Yes	No	"I often wonder if my spouse is working with me or against me."
Yes	No	"It seems that family rules are made to be broken."
Yes	No	"When my kids misbehave, I feel helpless."
Yes	No	"I blow my stack more than I'd like."
Yes	No	"My spouse and I fight over how to discipline the kids."
Yes	No	"Many of our family spats are over matters of principle."
Yes	No	"The kids are fully aware of how my spouse and I feel about things."
Yes	No	"I constantly second-guess the decisions I make over family matters."

No doubt you responded yes to several of the above items. Why do we feel out of control? The blend of personality styles, developmental levels, stress levels, emotional expressions, communication styles, and comfort levels often makes for a jarring mix. Most of us can contain our feelings about these differences as we deal with coworkers, friends and acquaintances, and extended family members. But once we pass over the threshold of our homes, our need to feel in control changes. One key fact causes us to struggle for control with immediate family members in ways we would not dare to with others: *We live through the lives of family members in an intimate way that does not characterize any other relationship.*

A mother who was also a teacher asked me a question that no doubt hounds many other family leaders. "Why," she asked, "am I able to control the kids in my classroom, but when I go home, I feel like a complete dolt when it comes to managing my family?"

"Because," I answered, "you don't live through your students as you do through your own children. Your kids are an extension of you in a way that your students are not."

We find it easier to give emotional space to those in whom we don't have a vested emotional interest. This teacher was capable of being objective with her students in a way that was more difficult with her husband and children.

But parents are not the only family members concerned about the issue of control. Children and teenagers struggle for control too. Take another test. This one deals with your children's thoughts. If you wish, ask your kids to help you respond to the following items, answering according to how they think. Again, respond yes or no to these statements:

Yes	No	"My parents constantly tell me what to do. They run my life."
Yes	No	"My parents say my anger is bad. You should see theirs!"
Yes	No	"All I want is to have some say in what happens to me."
Yes	No	"The reason I rebel is that nobody even tries to understand me."
Yes	No	"I get tired of my parents trying to tell me how I should think."
Yes	No	"I honestly think my parents don't know which side is up."
Yes	No	"I do some things for no other reason than to prove I can."

Yes   No   "If I don't like the rules, I don't follow them."

Yes   No   "Sometimes I have to be forceful just to get across my point."

Yes   No   "There are many things I refuse to discuss with my family."

Even though children are not the family leaders, they are not without means of taking over the control of the home. Your child may think several of the above thoughts. Though children may not voice their feelings aloud, they make their position abundantly clear.

Control can be negative or positive. When a basic human need, such as the need for control, is imbalanced, it demands attention. For example, a child who feels ignored tends to react with fear, even anger, to bring attention to this basic need. Unmet emotional needs come to the surface just as unmet physical urges do. The thirst for control is almost as strong as the thirst for water.

Being in control of one's world translates into security. It feels comfortable to know that the world is predictable. It feels good to know what is likely to happen next. A sense of calm prevails when family members feel protected from the world. Being in control pushes fear aside. It relieves anxiety. A world that is under control has order. It makes sense to us.

The apostle Paul enumerates a list of virtues as he writes, "The fruit of the Spirit is love, joy, peace, patience, kindness, goodness, faithfulness, gentleness and self-control" (Galatians 5:22-23). As psychologist Abraham Maslow has detailed, these virtues are not as powerfully driven as other more basic needs, such as hunger, thirst, sexual fulfillment, avoidance of pain, rest, and safety. If these more fundamental needs are not satisfied, a child, or even an adult, cannot satisfy higher level needs. Family members may become stuck as they seek fulfillment of one of these needs. Worse, they may develop tendencies such as harshness, argumentativeness, jealousy, angry outbursts, or defiance even though they have the natural capacity to give and receive affection. Note that Paul identifies many of these negative tendencies as "acts of the sinful nature" (see Galatians 5:19-21).

HOW DO YOUR FAMILY MEMBERS TRY TO CONTROL?

The struggle for control is central to many family problems. If families want to grow, they must understand the dynamics underlying the quest for control. All family members use different control tactics. What works for one family member may not work for another. Control tactics tend to match the individual's personality and stage of life. Notice the varied ways family members attempt to control their world:

- Intimidated by her children, a mother attempts to win them over by doing special favors.
- Uncomfortable talking about tender feelings, a husband barks at his wife rather than talks seriously about their faltering relationship.
- Ignored by her busy parents, a child develops chronic stomach pains that force her to miss school frequently.
- Convinced that he will be severely punished if he tells the truth, a teenager deceives his parents

about his role in a neighborhood vandalism scheme.

- Hoping to punish her husband for an earlier disagreement, a wife refuses to acknowledge his affectionate advances.
- Attempting to change a decision his family has made, a father provokes guilt in family members by predicting a gloomy outcome.

The ways family members attempt to control each other vary tremendously. Some individuals are competitive and aggressive. Others are quiet and subtle. Family members adjust their control tactics to their own strengths and weaknesses. But all people, regardless of age and status, enjoy the security of being in control of the world that surrounds them.

Children often do not feel a great deal of control over their home environment. In fact, many children are victimized by fearful circumstances. One common theme in family disputes is the struggle for control between parent and child. Insecure children will attempt to force control over their parents. Parents, in turn, may use silent control tactics to tell the child, "Please stop your worrying. Let me be in control of our family. If you don't willingly give me the reins of control, I will forcefully take them from you."

I advocate that children be reared in a structured and even somewhat protective home environment. Children, especially young children, need to be shielded from harmful experiences and others' mistakes. But as young people learn effective problem-solving and coping skills, parents should give them increased independence.

STRIKING THE BALANCE

Great damage occurs when either too few or too many controls exist in the home. Too much permissiveness frightens children, causing uncertainty. On the other hand, too much confinement prevents young people from gaining the needed experience to become independent. Balance between freedom and restriction is needed.

The same control dynamics that govern parent-child relationships spill over to the marriage relationship as well. While struggles for control take on a different dimension between adults, the underlying desire for security persists within the context of the marriage relationship. Many struggles between husbands and wives boil down to the same issues of security, predictability, freedom from fear, and independence that we see in adult-child struggles. A husband may want a guarantee that his wife values his position as family wage earner. A wife may desperately solicit affection from a withholding husband. The list of examples could go on endlessly. When an imbalance of power exists, tension is almost certainly present. That tension will be confronted in some fashion.

My father enjoys telling the story of a man who was quite certain that his marriage was good. After all, he and his wife seldom argued. She blindly accepted whatever the man said. She was quietly tolerant of his gruff ways. She met his every demand with appropriate respect. His wife seemed to understand that her role was to make him happy. If she had any hard feelings toward her husband, she certainly kept them to herself.

When a friend of this long-suffering wife asked how she managed to maintain her sanity while married to an overbearing, demanding ogre, the woman demurely responded, "Well, once a week, while my husband is at work, I clean the house. For years it has been my practice to clean the toilet in our bathroom with his toothbrush. That makes everything else tolerable."

GAINING CONTROL

Whether control tactics are blatant or subtle, all of us want to control our world. But try as we may, we cannot force control. If you feel caught in the middle of a power struggle, remember that beneath the controlling behavior is a person trying to find security. If your family members need help overcoming struggles for control, keep in mind these principles:

- Most family members resort to disturbing behaviors (e.g., arguing, whining, threats, intimidation) only after positive means of seeking security have failed.
- When family members give in to control tactics (e.g., by compromising, showing emotional hurt, counterattacking), they have, in effect, reinforced the likelihood that similar exchanges will take place in the future.
- In power struggles, family members are struggling over something other than what is outwardly apparent. The typical struggle for control is waged on a covert, emotional level.
- Efforts to force control over another usually are ineffective. To demand compliance from others only encourages those family members to search for ways to feel in control of themselves.
- People who have been repeatedly overpowered

by others tend to feel inadequate. By acting helpless, indifferent, withdrawn, or uninterested, those people are salvaging what little control they can.

- Families can avoid continual power struggles through communication that emphasizes honest emotional expression.
- Family members who engage others in struggles for control invariably have a need to feel comforted and affirmed.
- As family members gain a comfortable sense of control over those things under their direct power, their influence over others will increase.

Power struggles produce frustration. The people initiating the power struggle feel frustrated because even though they may win the war, things most often do not go smoothly. Most of us walk into emotional skirmishes hoping the other person sees things our way and will readily give in. And, of course, frustration abounds in the people who have been challenged. They did not want to scuffle in the first place. With a knee-jerk reaction, they typically offer what seems to be the most logical solution, hoping that the disagreement can be quickly and painlessly resolved. They are usually rebuffed, setting off a round of fruitless negotiations. When the struggle is between parents and children, the battle often ends in punishment. If the struggle is between adults, the resulting damage may be a different sort of punishment, like giving the silent treatment or passively refusing to cooperate or spreading rumors.

EMOTIONAL CONTROL

The most common question families ask about power struggles is this: *What do I do when one of my family members challenges me?* The answer may be dismaying: *There is nothing you can do to force victory in a power struggle.* Ugh! Not a particularly pleasant answer.

When trying to force compliance from a child, one punishment may be just as ineffective as another. There are no magical weapons parents can pull from their bag of tricks to force a child to act agreeably. Similarly, there is little a husband or wife can do to overpower the will of an unyielding spouse. To engage in underhanded maneuvers with a family member only ravages family unity. The use of force in family struggles always signals defeat. That's the bad news.

The good news is that you can maintain control in the home and actually win the power struggle if you do two things: give the other people the control they desire, and be consistent in your behavior.

Sound like surrender? It's not. Giving other people control is not the equivalent to yielding to their will. Most family members believe that when something is wrong with the family, they must fix it immediately. And, typically, we believe that we can't rely on the other family members to do the necessary repairs. We are convinced that job is ours.

But it is not. Once family members quit trying to fix each other's problems, solutions often emerge. Why? The people who own the problem cannot rely on someone else to solve their problem. That task has become theirs. For example:

- Toddlers or children may realize that you will not tell them how they should feel. You will set firm boundaries and show plenty of love. They must decide what they believe about themselves.

- Your teenagers know that you disagree with them on certain issues. Because you do not force them to believe as you do, they become more curious about your views. Your influence over them grows.

- A wife realizes that her husband supports her discipline of the children even though he would do things differently. She appreciates his tolerance and asks for his honest opinion of her family-management skills.

You give a family member control when you believe *I cannot force you to agree with me or feel the way I feel. I give you the freedom to choose how you will react, and I will exercise the freedom to choose how I will react. My choice is to remain in control of my emotions.*

Remember that a power struggle involves a struggle for *emotional* control, not behavioral control. When you decide to control your emotions rather than give them over to your challengers, you win the struggle by choosing not to fight. Your challengers can decide how they will control their own emotions.

Once you have determined that you are in charge of your emotions, you must follow through with a response. The family members challenging you are watching to see if you intend to do what you have said you will do. Will you hold tightly to your rule that your children are not to raid each other's closet? Will you do your daughter's homework or guide her as she does it? Will you continue to be a role model for the rest of your family?

Consistency in family relations simply means doing what you have said you would do. The family watches carefully to see if they can count on you to follow through with your stated plans. If you are inconsistent, they will challenge you. Consistency leaves less room for manipulation. The combination of emotional calm and consistent reactions serves as a winning combination in keeping families out of unhealthy power struggles.

DISCIPLINE THAT PREVENTS POWER STRUGGLES

Let's get practical. All parents have to discipline their children. But how can we discipline our children in ways that allow them to feel in control of themselves and that allow us to be consistent? Is it possible to separate discipline from ugly power struggles?

Think of the word *discipline*. Most of us equate discipline with a system of rewards and punishments. The aim of discipline is to *do* something that will teach the child right from wrong.

And that much is correct—partially.

But when we remember that one family member cannot force his or her will on another, we can quickly see that discipline involves so much more than teaching proper conduct. We must deal not only with inappropriate behavior but also with emotions. I suggest that this second factor is too often ignored in most family discipline plans. Hence, power struggles abound.

Recall that all behavior has a purpose. A three-year-old boy spits at his sister. There is a reason he did what he did. His mother reacts by punishing him. She may also give him a stern lecture. There is a reason for her behavior too—to make sure the child understands the seriousness of the offense. But to leave the disciplinary act at that is to deal with only half the problem. The child's emotions must also be addressed, for there is a reason he feels as he does. The message of discipline should be *I will deal with your behavior, but I will not ignore its underlying message.*

Family leaders must constantly choose when to confront inappropriate behavior. Several circumstances require a parent to confront the child:

- The child misbehaves and needs to be corrected.
- The child expresses an emotion inappropriately.
- The child shows poor judgment and needs redirection.
- The child ignores or violates the needs and rights of others.
- The child's personal growth is stunted because of irresponsibility.

The following two scenarios demonstrate situations that need disciplinary confrontation:

Situation: Two young sisters, Shelley and Kathy, have been playing with each other's toys and games. Neither really likes to let the other play with her things but does so only to gain access to the other's closet. Kathy has gotten into the bad habit of leaving Shelley's toys on her floor after playing with them, so Shelley has to pick them up. Fed up with Kathy, Shelley starts a shouting match that ends in an awful brawl.

Confrontation need: Kathy has violated her agreement with Shelley to return her toys to where she found them. Shelley is right to ask her sister to do what she had agreed to do, but in confronting Kathy, Shelley blasts her with hateful force. Their parents must do something to correct this misconduct. But strong feelings motivated the sisters to act as they did. Those feelings must be acknowledged for discipline to be effective.

Situation: Jim said he was going one place but went another. His parents were not only bothered by the fact that he deceived them, but they also were fearful that something could have gone wrong and they would not have known where their son was. They were concerned for his safety as much as they were bothered about his deceit.

Confrontation need: Jim placed himself in a potentially dangerous position. He needs to be taught the importance of integrity in relationships. His parents must do something to teach him to follow household rules and to be honest with others. Yet they should attend to the emotions behind Jim's deceit so that he does not feel the urge to sneak around his parents in similar situations.

CONFRONTATION THAT AVOIDS POWER STRUGGLES
Let's go a step further and look at ways to handle these disciplinary situations, taking into account the power struggles that underlie each circumstance. We will return to each situation and study how disciplinary action plus attention to underlying emotions makes an effective combination.

CASE STUDY: KATHY AND SHELLEY
Calling the girls into the family room, Dad asks, "What's the fuss about between you two?"

Defensively, Shelley accuses her sister. "Dad, I'm tired of Kathy playing with my things and then dropping them on my floor when she's through with them. Tell her to put them back where they belong!"

"Is that true, Kathy?" inquired Dad.

"Shelley does the same thing! Besides, she wouldn't let me put them up. She told me to get out of her room, so I just left her stuff and did what she told me."

Shelley reacted. "I didn't tell you to throw them on the floor. I told you to get out because—"

"Wait!" Dad interrupted. "I don't want to hear all that. I don't care who did what. Nobody plays with the other person's toys for the next week. Is that understood?"

At once both girls protested, but to no avail. Their dad would not listen to their argument. He had decided on a disciplinary action and intended to stick with it. When he sent the girls out of the room, they were mad—not only at each other but also at their dad for being so abrupt in announcing their punishment.

• • • •

At first glance, it seems that Shelley and Kathy's father has handled this disciplinary matter appropriately. He assessed the situation, made a quick decision, and exercised his disciplinary authority. He stayed out of an argument with his daughters, leaving little doubt about who was in control of the household. Mad or not, the girls got his message.

We may not find much room for complaint about this father's discipline, but if we take matters a step further, we can see how his dual positions as disciplinarian and family leader can be strengthened.

. . . .

Later in the evening, Dad called Shelley and Kathy back into the family room. He asked the girls, "How are things between you two? Everybody cooled off now?"

Both sisters nodded their heads. It had been more than an hour since their confrontation and their father's subsequent disciplinary action.

"Neither of you was too happy with the other when you left here. And I'm sure you didn't care for my decision to keep you from sharing your toys for a week."

Shelley was the first to speak up. "Dad, it's just that I think you punished me for something I didn't do. She's the one who threw my junk on my floor," she said, cocking her head sideways toward Kathy.

Kathy started to protect herself against her sister's accusation, but her dad quickly intervened. "I know each of you has an opinion about what happened. Shelley, you thought Kathy wasn't doing her part in taking care of your things, and Kathy, you felt Shelley shouted at you rudely. I want you to know, though, that I'm not so concerned with who's right and who's wrong. Both of you had reasons for feeling the way you did. I'm more interested in whether or not you two get along with one another. That's the point I'm emphasizing by disciplining you."

The girls stood silently before their father. Each wanted to resurrect the fight they had not finished, but they knew their dad would not allow it.

Dad continued, "I don't enjoy it when we're mad at each other. I know that you don't enjoy it either. My guess is that you're upset with me as much as you are each other."

By their silence, Shelley and Kathy affirmed their dad's suspicion.

"Do you have anything to say to me? What's been running through your minds?" Dad's voice suggested he was open to their comments.

Kathy was bold enough to speak her mind. "I think you're too strict. Why do you have to punish us?"

Dad nodded that he understood her feeling. He looked expectantly at Shelley. She added, "Sometimes I feel like you're mad at me when I don't feel that I've done anything wrong."

Dad clarified her observation, "You mean I don't understand what's running through you at the time?"

"Yes."

Again Dad nodded. He refrained from further remarks because he wanted to emphasize the girls' feelings and not his own. "Anything else?"

"Can't we decide when we can play with each other's things?"

Dad nodded his head affirmatively. "I've got no prob-lem with that—after next week." He smiled warmly and added, "I know that's not exactly what you wanted to hear, but that's where we stand." He touched each girl on the shoulder and added, "I hope that we won't have too many more arguments." The brief discussion ended, and the girls went their separate ways.

• • • •

Although it may seem that this father's comments stirred his daughters' irritation because he refused to back down from his earlier decision, he actually elevated himself in their eyes. Children are notorious for their complaints about strict parents. Truth is, though, kids like a household that is predictable in a way that also protects their dignity.

By bringing his children's feelings to the forefront, this father was acknowledging his children's privilege to feel the way they felt. In essence, he communicated, "I will take disciplinary action to teach you right from wrong, but I will not attempt to control your feelings. It will be up to you to do that." That communication helped to solidify his standing as a family leader, without diminishing his role as an understanding dad.

CASE STUDY: JIM'S DECEIT

When Jim returned home, his mother asked him to sit and have a soft drink with her. "Jim, I found out from Mrs. Richardson that you were at the park instead of her house, as you had told us." Jim's head immediately dropped as if pulled in that direction by his own shame.

With no judgment in her voice, she continued, "You know we don't want you to go to the park unless an adult goes with you. You must have thought you could go and we'd never find out."

Bingo. Jim's eyes crept slightly upward as he stole a quick glance at his mom, wondering how she had read his mind.

"I'm not mad at you. I know you thought you would be safe. But since you did what you did, you have to stay home the rest of the day. And the next time you go out, I'll check on you to make sure you go where you tell me you're going."

Jim's face assumed an injured look. He wanted to argue with his mother, and he would have, but she got up from her chair and started to fix lunch. Later in the afternoon, his mother took him outside and shot baskets with him for about half an hour.

••••

Just as Kathy and Shelley's father had done, Jim's mother balanced her dual roles as family leader and communicator. She was bold enough to voice what she knew Jim was thinking and refrained from judging his poor decision. She knew that he was fully aware of her disapproval. By doing so, she left Jim's honor intact. He was given no reason to feel belittled, demeaned, insulted, or discredited. When she pronounced her disciplinary verdict, the focus was on his behavior and not his character. She proved her lack of condemnation by playing basketball with him later in the day, though she did not budge from her punishment.

Jesus' relationships with his disciples showed us that he relied on the strength of relationships to increase his influence over others. For example, when Jesus spoke harshly to Peter, he did so with the knowledge that their friendship was on sound footing (John 13:36-38). Later, he took the chance to restore Peter's dignity (John 21:15-23). Jesus taught two lessons in his interactions with Peter: Jesus could confront Peter about his inappropriate behavior, and Jesus could help Peter grow by understanding him and by bringing healing to their relationship. That concept can be applied to the family. As we discipline our children, we must remember that forging a strong relationship does more to influence a child than mere punishment.

Summary: We all need to feel as if we are in control of our corner of the world. But sometimes a family member's need to control causes a power struggle in the family. When that happens, remember that the power struggle itself is not necessarily the issue. What's important is the message behind the power struggle. The fight for control is often the signal that a family member is insecure. Some of the struggle will dissipate when we fill that need for security. But other power struggles will call for confrontation. When parents initiate a confrontation, they must remember two things: the only person we can control is ourselves, and we must act consistently. We can exert influence in our families if we respond not only to the troublesome behavior but also to the emotions and needs that lie beneath the behavior.

1. One of the most important truths family members should live by is this: *The only person in the entire world I can control is me. I cannot force control on others. I can only influence them.* In our enthusiasm to ensure our children's growth, we may unintentionally violate this principle. Here are some thoughts on this idea of replacing influence for control:

- Even healthy parent-child relationships can be surprisingly frustrating. We want to help, and we feel guilty that we cannot do more.
- Children never ask parents foolish questions, only questions to dilemmas they have yet to solve.
- When parents give children all the answers, children quit thinking. When families have discussions, children never quit thinking.
- A parent's influence over a child depends not on how much the parent knows about the child but on how well the parent understands.
- Children instinctively know what lies in their inner heart. They need a parent's help to look deeper.
- The more you understand God, the more you understand yourself. You can then be a stronger friend to your family.
- Children learn from their mistakes. They learn

even more from their parents' responses to their mistakes.
- Children change. Parents change. God never changes. His strength is what makes families grow.
- Once children are convinced that parents and other people understand their hearts, they will hear and welcome helpful suggestions.
- Children carry the fruits of family relationships wherever they go. Use good fertilizer.

2. In 1 Corinthians 13, the apostle Paul offers the antithesis for family power struggles. Where the qualities of love abound, contention is quieted. Note the qualities of love Paul enumerates. Love is long-suffering, kind, and humble. Paul also names the actions of love. Love behaves politely, considers others' needs, holds its temper, thinks wholesome thoughts, delights in the truth, and is constant. Think back to three power struggles you have faced in your family in the last month. Think of how you might handle those situations differently now. Replay those struggles in your mind, this time acting firmly in love and with understanding. Ask God to give you the wisdom to handle the next family power struggle with new insight.

3. Read each of the following descriptions of a family member's behavior. Examine the potential dynamics of that situation, and identify ways the person may be using behaviors and emotions to force control onto his or her relationships.

Situation: Nine-year-old Marsha is normally a coopera-tive child. She wants to win other people's approval. Recently, however, she has missed several days of school. In the mornings, she seems to be genuinely ill, but as the day progresses, it is evident that her illness has passed. When questioned by her mother, she can-not offer an explanation for her sickness other than to say she truly felt sick.

- In what ways is Marsha controlling her family?
- How would you respond to Marsha's control?

Situation: Wesley is a husband and father of three chil-dren. He and his brother own and operate their own small business. Wesley's wife and children have asked him to spend more time at home, but he insists he must work long hours. Wesley knows that he could hire a manager to relieve some of his workload, but he does not want to. He enjoys his family, but he receives even greater satisfaction from his work.

- In what ways is Wesley controlling his family?
- How would you respond to Wesley's control?

Situation: Lydia admits that she is something of a perfec-tionist. It is important that the house be kept in neat order. She frequently chides her children and husband when they fail to live up to what she considers to be ac-ceptable standards of cleanliness. Her family tells her she is nagging them. She claims she is not.

- In what ways is Lydia controlling her family?
- How would you respond to Lydia's control?

CHAPTER TEN

Value Each Other

THE woman hung her head low as her husband stood over her. She said nothing to him, although her entire body was full of emotion. If she could only speak up, she could gorge the air with feelings. But to force any words from her heart to her mouth was impossible.

"Well, what do you have to say about that?" barked the man, referring to the way his wife had handled their children just moments earlier. The daughter had meekly asked for help on a simple project that was too tough for her six-year-old mind to comprehend. The stress-laden mother had blasted her for being so inept that she could not manage the simplest of tasks without help. The son, practically a man at age nine, had come to his sister's aid. His efforts were fruitless. He was leveled with the mother's flawed judgment just as his sister had been. He became the target of his mother's warped discipline, absorbing several blows from the distraught woman.

Hearing the commotion, the husband, playing the role of the family superhero, quickly assumed the position of policeman. Secretly he relished the chance to put his wife in her place yet one more time. He held her in contempt and needed only the slightest excuse to shellac her with his brand of male superiority. In the presence of the children, he yanked up his wife as he would an ill-behaved puppy and virtually thrashed her into submission. He felt completely justified in his action because she had attacked his children. The man told his wife that she was an abuser, and she was inclined to believe him. Slumping before him in a chair that was about as worn as her self-esteem, she could think of no defense for her behavior. She could not think at all.

Only seconds after asking his wife to explain herself, the man grew livid with rage and screamed again, "Tell me why! Why do you treat these kids the way you do? Do you want me to treat you the same way you treat them? It doesn't feel good, you know!"

In a pleading voice, the woman shouted back at her husband, "I can't tell you why I do anything. I only know that I hate myself! I hate myself for the way I treat these children. And I hate myself for the way I treat *me*. And I hate you too!"

• • • •

"Mom, can we change the channel?" Peter took his gaze off the television set and stared at his mother.

"No problem. That show was getting pretty bad. I don't know why they put such trash on television. The show could have been good, but then they had to drag up that awful confrontation between the husband and his wife to put some drama into it. I wish they wouldn't do that."

"Was that man going to hit his wife?" the child asked, curious about the show they had been watching.

"Who knows? Probably. It looks as if the story was headed in that direction." She shook her head and silently reprimanded herself for letting her seven-year-old son see as much of the television program as he had. She did not want him to get the wrong impression of what normal family life was like.

Later in the evening, as Peter lay in bed, his mother came in to say good-night. "Mom, why do people act like that?"

"Like what, Son?"

"You know, the way that woman acted to her children on television and the way that man treated her. He scared me."

Peter's mom took advantage of his questions to teach a lesson about family life. "I am sorry I let you watch that program, Peter. The parents in that family didn't value each other or their children very much. What I mean is that the mother didn't like herself very much, Peter. That's why she was so edgy with her children. And her husband probably didn't feel too good about himself either. That's why he was so mean to his wife. Sad, isn't it?"

Peter nodded his head in agreement. "I'm just glad you and Dad aren't like that. I'm glad you like each other and me."

SELF-ESTEEM DEFINES FAMILY RELATIONSHIPS

Peter's mother was correct when she explained that the way mothers and fathers feel about themselves plays an important role in how they treat each other and their children. Our behavior serves as a message board, proclaiming just how we feel about ourselves. Consider the following examples of how adult behavior reflects the person's self-esteem:

• An uncertain mother worries constantly that her children will fall prey to all of life's traps. She perpetually hounds the kids to bundle up before they go outside, to eat all the food on their plates, to use their best manners with friends, or to study hard so they can make something of their adult life. Her concern is legitimate, but it is overworked. Her own self-doubt pushes her to prevent similar shortcomings in her children.

• An aloof father talks to his family only when he has something negative to say. He reprimands the children for their wrongdoing but ignores their achievements. He complains to his wife about trivial matters but is seldom willing to work with her to solve problems. His fear of being close to others makes it easy to withdraw from meaningful contact with his family, even though he grumbles about the lack of family communication.

• A confident mother is bothered, but not ruffled, when her children bring home disappointing grades from school. She looks for ways to encourage the kids for what they have done right, but she also tries to figure out how they may have slipped through the loopholes to make poor grades. Once she feels she has a good handle on the problem, she makes adjustments in her supervision of the children's homework. She has confidence that they will adjust to her efforts to work more closely with their teachers.

• A successful businessman recognizes that the approach he has used to make his business succeed works with his family just as it does with his employees. He pays close attention to the small things his family does right and openly acknowledges even small improvements. Just as he surprises productive workers with unexpected rewards, he seizes chances to compliment his wife and children. He takes advantage of the power of positive attention whenever he can.

The self-esteem of family leaders influences how their children develop. Children enter this world with a blueprint for personality. To a large degree, their behavioral tendencies are determined by this inborn disposition. But as children interact with their world, and especially with their families, their personalities take shape. The development of young children's self-esteem plays a crucial role in their character development.

Parents are the single most important figures in the development of children's self-esteem. In the following illustrations, note how the children's interpretation of themselves is swayed by their parents:

• A three-year-old boy is told that big boys do not cry. The parents' intent is to convince the youngster that there are better ways to influence others than by whining and sobbing. In his innocence, the boy comes to believe that he is bad when he cries. He learns that he is better off simply to keep his feelings to himself.

• An eight-year-old girl is teased when she tells her family that she intends to play football on the high school team when she is old enough. Her brother chides her for thinking so foolishly. Her dad tells her that she needs to set more realistic goals. Her mom explains that life restricts the choices a female can make. In the end the girl doubts her own sense of judgment. She thought she knew her strengths, but now she is unsure of herself.

• A teenager gives in and smokes a cigarette with a friend. His guilt convinces him to confess to his parents. Recognizing the strength it must have taken him to admit to this act, his mother tells him that even though she disagrees with his choice of behavior, she is pleased that he was bold enough to come to her with his mistake. The young man concludes that his mother is someone he can trust to help him learn from his mistakes.

• A preschooler tells her daddy that she's afraid to go to school the next day. She knows she will have a new teacher and is unsure if this teacher can live up to her high expectations as the last one did. Her dad knows that it is his daughter's task, not his, to decide what she thinks of the new situation. He tells her, "I'll be interested to hear what you think of the new teacher. I'll make sure to ask you about it as soon as I get home tomorrow." Though still uncertain, the child surmises that she will have to face whatever uncertainties the next day holds for her.

SELF-ESTEEM NEEDS CHANGE AS LIFE CHANGES
As family leaders try to help family members develop positive self-esteem, they need to understand that self-esteem needs change as children develop. Young children look primarily to their parents for the satisfaction of their self-esteem needs. Teens still need family input, but they begin to rely more heavily on peer relationships to offer them a sense of worth. Adults receive support from each other, but they also look for the approval of their children as proof that they are of value. Note how self-esteem needs change as life changes.

Birth to five years

- Infants look to their parents, especially their mothers, for a sense of safety and security.
- Young children are almost completely dependent on parents to satisfy personal and emotional needs.
- Trust (or mistrust) in others develops as a by-product of family interactions.
- Young children define themselves by absorbing the emotional reactions of their family.
- Young children test their world, concluding from parents' discipline efforts whether they are capable of acting independently.

Ages six to twelve

- As children compare themselves to other children, they draw conclusions about their social competence.
- Children try new skills and measure their competence by their ability to compete with others.
- Children actively seek input from parents about their personal adequacy.
- Children search for the best way to express their feelings, noting their successes and failures in relationships.

Adolescent years

- Teenagers look to their peer group as the primary source of approval or rejection.
- Teenagers take on various roles as they struggle to define their personal identities.
- Self-esteem is partially, if not largely, defined by appearance.

- Success in dealing with the opposite sex builds or ravages feelings of personal worth.
- Parental reactions to awkward adolescent maneuvering affects inner confidence.

Adulthood

- The intimacy of adult relationships, especially the marriage relationship, contributes to feelings of value.
- Personal and family achievements enrich healthy pride.
- Giving meaningfully to others becomes a greater source for self-gratification.
- Achieving vocational goals helps adults feel that they are "somebody."
- The ability to make sense of the past, replete with both success and failure, gives a sense of closure as well as motivation for the future.

Self-esteem cannot grow in a vacuum. We each need others to help us define ourselves. Young children's self-esteem can be given a jump start by parents' efforts to provide for both physical and emotional needs. Teenagers—though they are convinced they no longer need parents—can benefit from the patient response of parents who say, "We will give you the space you need to be your own person, but we will also give you the support to prop you up when you make mistakes." Even adults rely on the family for continued self-esteem growth, though as people grow older, they assume more personal responsibility for their progress. Achievements in adult life can provide only so much gratification. Success in relationships gives an adult a greater sense of accomplishment than any other type of victory.

TAKING CHARGE OF YOUR SELF-ESTEEM

Take the following test to chart your own self-esteem growth through the years. The first set of statements deals with the way you felt when you were a child and teenager. The second set helps you see your current view of yourself.

Answer yes or no to the statements about your life as a child and/or teenager:

Yes	No	Other kids picked on me a lot.
Yes	No	I had a hard time making and keeping friends.
Yes	No	I was easily embarrassed or shamed.
Yes	No	I gave my parents and/or teachers a lot of trouble.
Yes	No	I had no one I could really confide in.
Yes	No	I often felt left out of my peer group.
Yes	No	I had a hard time adjusting to changes, even relatively small changes.
Yes	No	I felt that I was not as nice looking as the other kids.
Yes	No	I failed to receive the kind of attention I needed.
Yes	No	I kept to myself much of the time.
Yes	No	I had no one at home to turn to when my feelings were hurt.
Yes	No	I exaggerated my problems in order to get attention.

Yes　No　I frequently told lies or covered the truth to avoid criticism.

Yes　No　I took far too many risks.

Yes　No　I had a hard time trusting others.

Answer yes or no to the following statements about the way you feel about yourself right now:

Yes　No　I argue a lot with the people I love most.

Yes　No　I find myself questioning other people's motives.

Yes　No　I have a hard time making decisions and sticking to them.

Yes　No　My feelings are easily hurt.

Yes　No　People tell me I'm not objective in the way I view others.

Yes　No　I am easily intimidated by others, especially forceful people.

Yes　No　I can't stand criticism, even if it is meant to be helpful.

Yes　No　I feel guilty when I stand up for my own needs.

Yes　No　I tend to be a reactor instead of an initiator.

Yes　No　I admit I am my own worst critic.

Yes　No　I feel obligated to try to solve my friends' problems.

Yes　No　I often doubt if others really want to know my opinion.

Yes　No　Others seem to "have it together" more than I do.

Yes　No　I have trouble opening up to others for fear of what they will think.

It is satisfying to hear an adult say, "When I was younger, I had a pretty low opinion of myself, but now that I'm an adult, I've discovered that I'm not such a bad person." Conversely, it is discouraging to hear an adult say, "I didn't like myself much when I was a child, and I still don't."

Self-esteem development can be broken into two simple stages: childhood (birth to age eighteen), when children base their self-concept on what they absorb from the world around them; and adulthood (age eighteen and beyond), when people have the capacity to determine what they think about themselves.

Sometimes it seems that life works in backward progression. Countless times adults have said to me, "I want to reconstruct my self-esteem, but the damage done when I was young was so extensive, I'll never overcome it." They are disquieted that by the time they reach an age when they can play an active role in shaping their own self-concept, heavy damage has already been done by abusive adults, demeaning siblings, or coldhearted peers. These adults go on to say that if they could make one change in their lives, it would be to give their self-esteem a complete face-lift.

I have to admit that I have often wondered why God would allow life to be so harsh on people, especially children. I ask if it is fair that some adults feel as low and depressed about life as they do simply because they were emotionally damaged during their formative years. Because I am convinced that God is loving and not cruel, I find myself searching for answers that match this positive view of our Creator.

I am reminded that the construction of self-esteem is a lifelong project. Though the framework is assembled during early childhood, the project is never fully completed. I believe that God never intends us to reach a point at which we say, "I am perfectly developed. This is all there is to my life." He wants more for each of us. He wants us to keep growing.

If we believe that God's plan for our lives is perfect—and I do—then we must also believe that he requires us to be his partners in working out that plan. My job, and yours, is to take what life has given us during the early years, accept its influence on the shaping of our self-concept, and make the adjustments we can at this stage of our lives.

Too often we want God to solve all our problems, and we resist being a part of the solution. Perhaps that was the case when the earliest Christians gathered in Jerusalem for the first day of Pentecost following Christ's death. The Acts 2 account of this momentous day tells of some spectacular acts that occurred that day. The event was something anyone would want to experience. The writer tells us, "All of them were filled with the Holy Spirit" (Acts 2:4). We are led to believe that this episode forever changed the lives of the thousands of people who experienced it.

What happened on that festive day was not a one-time occurrence. Look at the elements in place that day, and notice how any of us can experience a similar encounter. First, past experiences had traumatized these people, causing them to despair. Second, these people held a glimmer of hope that God could still work in their midst; despite their despair, they had not completely given up on life. Third, rather than hope that God would miraculously rescue them from the awful experiences they had had, these people were willing to let God work through them; *they became a part of God's solution to overcoming their own past trauma.*

We can learn from the experiences of these early Christians. Note how the Pentecost experience can speak to us when we struggle with self-esteem problems. First, past experiences may have had a traumatizing effect on the way we feel about ourselves, creating feelings of disillusionment or despair. Second, we may feel caught in a trap, hoping that God—anyone—will rescue us; we are looking for an external solution. Third, life-changing experiences occur when we become internally involved in finding solutions to life's past tragedies; God then fills us with the strength to live in harmony with ourselves and other people.

THE CYCLICAL NATURE OF EMOTIONAL NEEDS

A task of the family leader is to help family members understand that personal growth never ends. The family is a network. For any system or network to function adequately, all parts must work together. In a family system, all family members must keep growing in their understanding of themselves and each other. All parts of the system are interdependent. A healthy interdependence among family members will build each person's sense of self-worth.

Take a look at this interaction between a husband and wife, Sharon and Willard, from a counseling session. They are trying to generate ideas of how they could disengage from hurtful emotional struggles by helping one another grow in their self-worth:

> *Counselor:* Let's get specific about what can be done to help each other build self-esteem.

> *Wife:* I can tell you what I want.

> *Husband:* What?

> *Wife:* I just want us to spend more time together, the way we used to. We get so hung up on doing things with the kids that we forget about ourselves. Willard, I just want to talk to you! You hardly even know what I think about things.

> *Counselor:* It's not that you want to talk about problems all the time. You just want to share yourself with Willard. That makes you feel that you're important to him.

> *Husband:* I can buy that. But I'll tell you what I need. I need space when I've made a mistake. I know when I've done wrong, and I don't need someone to point out all my faults.

> *Counselor:* If we could count the number of positive and negative comments you make to each other daily, I wonder what the ratio would be. Ideally, the positive would far outnumber the negative.

> *Husband (laughing):* I'd be scared to count.

Wife: I'm going to say something, and I hope it's taken the right way. Willard, when you say nice things to me or when you touch me, I know exactly what you're after. It's just a part of foreplay.

Counselor: Willard's kindness means more to you when you know there are no strings attached.

Wife: That's exactly what I mean. It seems that everything we do, he turns it into a competition. He's trying to achieve something, even if it's to "make time" with me.

Husband: So what's the point? What are you getting at?

Wife: The point is that I don't want you to pursue me constantly. I want you just to enjoy being with me! That's what makes me feel good about myself— to know that you want my companionship.

Husband: Well, how about if we do things away from home? Maybe you won't be so suspicious of me then. We could go sailing sometime—just the two of us.

Counselor: Or you could go out on a date occasionally, the way you probably did before children came along. There are plenty of options to choose from. And as your relationship with each other grows, your positive feelings about yourselves will grow too.

In a short time, this couple developed a plan of action to include ways each could help the other feel fulfilled. They arranged a regular time to talk about the day-to-day matters that concerned their family. They pledged to decrease complaints and criticism and increase compliments and pleasant remarks toward each other. They spent more time doing things they both enjoyed doing. They committed to touch one another several times daily in a nonsexual manner. And they planned to go out on a date at least once a month. Note the comments this husband and wife made at the end of their session:

> **Wife:** I came in here today wanting to talk about what Willard and I should do to keep the boys from constantly fighting with each other. We ended up talking about our relationship. If I'm going to be any kind of mother at all, I've got to feel good about being *me*. Maybe the next time we can spend more time on the kids. I don't want to neglect their needs. They are the real reason this family needs counseling.

> **Counselor:** Depending on how you look at it, we *did* talk about things that will impact your boys. After all, they derive a lot of their self-worth from you. And the way they feel about themselves has a lot to do with the way they attempt to force their feelings on others. It would be difficult at best for them to feel good about who they are if their

mother and father are struggling with their own relationship.

Husband: I suppose they depend on us having a good marriage. We know it, but it's easy to forget that fact. I know I feel good about myself if I'm doing something that counts. I understand what Sharon's saying about how she wants us to spend time just hanging around each other. I know we need that. I've got to adjust my thinking.

Counselor: The whole family depends on one another. The self-esteem of one family member can't be completely separated from the rest of the family. When one person feels ignored, that person's self-esteem may suffer. And you can't separate the way you act from the way you feel about yourself.

• • • •

Family needs move in cycles. The same emotional needs that were important during the formative years, such as self-esteem development, persist in adulthood. The expression of a need may change its shape as time passes, but the need remains nonetheless. I like to view people's emotional makeup as being similar to their physical stature. The child's body is small and needs to be properly nourished for it to grow. When children become adults, they do not have the same physical needs as when they were younger, but to assume that the body no longer requires attention would be a mistake.

Similarly, a child's need to feel valued continues into

adulthood. Of course, the way this need is adequately met is different from how it was met years earlier. To ignore the need to feel valued, though, would produce emotional damage. Family leaders who are sensitive to the needs of all family members (no small task!) help the family move away from struggles toward family balance.

Parents can help their children develop a healthy sense of self-worth by

- providing a warm and friendly home atmosphere
- spending regular time talking about things that interest family members
- offering acceptance and positive instruction when people make mistakes
- focusing on positive improvements instead of negative setbacks
- controlling emotions when discipline must be administered
- taking time to relate spiritual truths to daily dilemmas

Adults can also help one another grow in their feelings of self-worth by

- tenderly touching one another regularly
- listening to each other's frustrations without feeling the urge to criticize
- taking time out from the daily routine to relax and have fun
- giving words of encouragement when stress attacks family life

- admitting mistakes without feeling the need to make excuses
- surprising one another with unannounced gestures of courtesy or respect

Summary: We never outgrow our need for developing healthy self-esteem. While the needs of children and adults differ, we all need contact with others, companionship, reassurance, praise, friendship, physical touch, and recognition. A family is the best place to develop a secure sense of self. Parents who value each other and themselves have the greatest chance of seeing their children grow in their self-esteem. Even if parents were emotionally damaged when they were children, with God's help, they can grow into people with a healthy sense of worth. As we learn to value each other, our families will grow into interdependent networks that cultivate growth and unity.

Part 3 has helped us explore two key questions that influence our families: Who's in control? and How do we build self-esteem? Part 4 will demonstrate how building healthy family communication and maintaining a strong marriage will help our families grow.

1. Take time during the next few days to do one or more of the following self-esteem-building activities with your children:

- Do one of your children's chores for them.
- Take your kids out for ice cream after supper and let them buy the big cone.
- Surprise your children with a dollar bill after catching them doing something good.
- Ask your children what they would like for supper, and fix it for the entire family.
- Play kickball in the backyard or in a park.
- Sit on the edge of your child's bed and listen as he or she tells you about the day.

2. Take time during the next few days to do one or more of the following self-esteem-building activities with your spouse:

- Give your spouse a back rub.
- Go on a date.
- Fix supper for the family if you normally do not.
- Tell your spouse you will complete any chore he or she requests by the weekend.
- Hold hands for at least five minutes.
- Write down ten positive characteristics of your spouse and post them on the refrigerator.

3. Select a circumstance that has been a topic of discussion in your home: for example, a father's drinking problem, a mother's chronic anxiety, relentless sibling rivalry, children's disobedience, parents' arguments.

- On a piece of paper, write the emotions you suspect each member of your family experiences as a result of that difficult circumstance. You may find that there are many overlapping feelings among family members.
- Place yourself again in the shoes of each family member and ask yourself: How does this family member try to control this situation? What impact does this circumstance have on this family member's self-esteem? How does our family's discomfort affect each member's motivation to change? Write down your answers.
- Do you notice any patterns that show how each of you satisfies his or her need to feel important through interdependence? What are those patterns? What power struggles are recurrent? Is your family aware of how each person can potentially help the others realize their God-given value?

4. What issues do you feel your family should discuss in a family conference? How can you help each other recognize that every member of your family has equal value and worth?

PART **FOUR**

*Set the Tone for
Family Growth*

CHAPTER ELEVEN

Learn to Communicate

I HOPE that the preceding chapters have helped you begin to understand why your family members act as they do. And I hope that this understanding has led to some significant growth in your entire family.

As family leaders, we have a responsibility and the opportunity to set the tone for our families to grow. These last two chapters will explore two important ways that we can make sure the climate in our homes will help each family member develop: establishing healthy communication and maintaining a strong marriage.

Most of us agree that our families need to communicate more effectively. When family members are asked to list their family's communication problems, adult family members might say:

- "We argue over how to handle the kids."
- "I'll say one thing, and then he contradicts me by saying the opposite."
- "She doesn't care about my feelings. She just says what she thinks."
- "Whenever he talks, you can almost see the sarcasm dripping from his mouth."
- "Somehow I feel guilty when I tell them what I really think."
- "When she gets mad, she makes threats about what she's going to do."

Children and teenagers have their own ideas about family communication. Note some of the things they say:

- "Just because I'm a kid, I never have a say in what goes on around here."
- "Everybody drags up the past, as if I can change that!"
- "My parents make me talk nice to them, but you should hear how they talk to me."
- "I'm always in the middle of my parents' fights. I wish they would leave me out!"
- "When I cry or get upset, they tell me to quit crying—as if I can just shut off my feelings."
- "I'm afraid to say what I really feel because my parents make me feel two inches tall. I can't stand the guilt."

COMMUNICATION BEGINS
WITH UNDERSTANDING OURSELVES

We think of communication as a natural activity. We all do it. One family member talks, and another answers.

One gestures, and another motions back. One acts, the other reacts. The formula seems so simple, easy to follow.

But is it?

Whether or not we realize it, we all follow guidelines as we communicate with one another—call them rules if you wish—and not all families function under the same rules. What is acceptable to one family is taboo in another. We probably cannot trace the origins of most family rules. We do what we do because—well, just because.

Read the following list of rules some families follow as they communicate with one another, and see if you recognize any of these as unspoken rules in your family:

- Stick to the subject, and don't bring up the past. It's dead and shouldn't be resurrected.
- If you can't say something nice, then don't say anything at all.
- Everyone should be allowed to say what he or she feels, even if it is negative.
- There are no wrong answers, just wrong attitudes.
- Wait until your anger has passed before you talk because anger will ruin a good conversation.
- Whatever you say, keep it short and simple.
- No double-talk. Say what you mean, and mean what you say.
- It never hurt anyone to say "I'm sorry" or "I love you."
- Tell me if you've done wrong. It's better to hear it from you than from someone else.

You can no doubt add to this list of communication rules. We all know hundreds of them. By the time children reach school age, even they can recite a long list of such rules. The problem is that while families know the ways of healthy communication, they have such a hard time following them.

Why is that so?

Effective communication is hard to achieve. Effective communication involves more than understanding a set of rules: It involves understanding others' emotional needs. This point has been emphasized throughout this book, but it bears continued repeating. Before we can fully understand others, though, we must be aware of our own communication tendencies.

Let's take another test to appraise your understanding of healthy family-communication techniques. Answer yes or no to each of the following statements according to your usual way of communicating with family members. Be as honest as you can be with yourself.

Yes　No　My family feels that I am an understanding person.

Yes　No　I generally consider the timing of the statements I make.

Yes　No　I withhold a comment if I think it will hurt someone's feelings.

Yes　No　I would rather end an argument than get in the last word.

Yes　No　I pay more attention to the other person's feelings than to who's winning the argument.

Yes　No　I'm good at looking at alternative points of view.

Yes　No　I do a good job of avoiding verbal jabs that hurt.

Yes   No   I'm quick to apologize or say I'm sorry for what I've done wrong.

Yes   No   I am usually gracious when I accept a family member's apology.

Yes   No   When I offer constructive criticism, my comments are short and sweet.

Yes   No   I may get angry, but I do a good job of controlling my emotions.

Yes   No   I realize that destructive humor and sarcasm have no place in an argument.

Yes   No   If I tell my family I will do something, I follow through with my promise.

Yes   No   I keep private matters private.

Yes   No   What happened in the past is over. I see no need to resurrect old problems.

Yes   No   I try to avoid comments that begin with "You always" or "You never."

Yes   No   I see no need to say things that will only make my family feel guilty.

Yes   No   Once an argument is over, I try to put it behind me and move on with life.

Yes   No   I try hard to let the other person make his or her point before I respond.

Yes   No   I'm good at working out compromises.

Yes   No   When a family member is talking, I try to imagine what that person is feeling at that very moment.

Yes   No   I view every member of our family to be completely equal.

Yes   No   I use physical touch as a way of communicating my feelings to my family.

Yes   No   There are virtually no topics I refuse to discuss in our home.

Yes   No   If I see that I am making others
uncomfortable, I ease up.

Yes   No   I try hard to be open and honest with
myself and my family.

After completing this test, do two things. First, tally the number of "no" responses you made. Obviously, the higher this number, the greater your need to work on your communication style. Communication begins with an understanding of your own style of relating to family members. Second, ask your spouse and children to evaluate the way you have rated yourself. They may not agree with your self-appraisal. If your family believes you are lacking in certain communication areas, target those areas for improvement.

One factor that makes family leaders effective communicators is a thorough understanding of themselves. This understanding covers such issues as personal values, goals, spiritual beliefs, emotional tendencies, likes and dislikes, personality traits, and so on. As we know ourselves and feel comfortable with our own progress in life, we will be more effective family guides. The responses we offer will reflect that confidence, resulting in smoother family relations.

THE HIDDEN NATURE OF COMMUNICATION

As we have said before in this book, 90 percent of communication is nonverbal. While that alone is astounding, communication experts also tell us that of the actual words we speak, most have hidden, covert messages attached.

Note the complex circuit of energy that sweeps between two people as they communicate:

- The sender's words are accepted by the receiver.
- The receiver carefully notices the sender's tone of voice, body movements, and gestures. The receiver may not even be aware that he or she is processing the nonverbal signals.
- The receiver tries to mesh the sender's words and actions together so that they make sense.
- The sender carefully observes the receiver to determine if the message was accurately absorbed.
- The receiver considers the context in which the message was sent as he or she attempts to interpret it.
- The receiver arrives at a conclusion about what the sender meant and decides how to respond.
- The sender awaits a reply, poised to process the upcoming response.

You were probably unaware that communication was so complicated. Little wonder communication breaks down so often. So much takes place between two people during a simple conversation. Family members often miss the hidden implication of the message. Note the veiled meanings beneath the following words:

Boy: My dad never says anything but no. I hate him!

Hidden message: I'd give anything if my dad would tell me he loves me.

Mother: If you keep making threats like that, one of these days somebody's going to accept your challenge. Then what are you going to do?

251

Hidden message: I'm worried that you're burning your bridges with others. You need relationships more than you realize.

Father: I've just about had it with all of you! I've a good mind to leave through that door and never come home again!

Hidden message: I'm so depressed that I've just about given up hope. I want us to be close to one another rather than so distant.

Girl: Get out of my room. You're never to step foot in here again!

Hidden message: I want to feel in control of my small corner of the world.

We all know the rules of communication, but we often willingly break them. Interestingly enough, when people break the rules, they often do so with the faint hope that someone will recognize their underlying feelings. Family members may wish to call attention to a burning need. They may be trying desperately to reason with a loved one who is about to make a mistake. They may be crying out for affection or appreciation. They may be asserting an emotional need. Whatever the reason, most family members break the rules of communication for a good reason.

LISTENING IS THE MOST IMPORTANT COMMUNICATION TOOL

I would guess that most frustrated family members complain that no one else in the home understands them.

During your next family argument, listen for the words *You just don't understand.* If they are not actually spoken, they will be implied. In the following scenario, notice how the perceived lack of understanding between a mother and daughter pushes the following conversation over the edge.

Situation: Ellie Barker looked her daughter squarely in the eye, trying to force respect from the girl. Snapping at the child, she said, "Gwen, I just don't get it. You treat your father so disrespectfully. Why, when I was thirteen years old, my daddy died. I didn't go through my teenage years with someone to guide me. You have a father who loves you, and you don't even give him the time of day. I don't get it! You don't treat me any better either."

Gwen shook her head in disgust. It seemed natural for her to wag her head from side to side; she did it so often. "Mom, you just don't understand. I know you didn't have your father around for too long. But did he treat you the way Dad treats me? I doubt it. Your dad didn't hit you and then call it a spanking, did he? How can I act as if I love him? I can't do that. Too much has gone on between Dad and me. You've just got to give me time!"

Ellie almost rolled her eyes but quickly caught herself. No use making her daughter madder than she already was. Trying to sound logical, the mother replied, "Maybe Dad is rough on you kids. I'll admit that. But you never give him a chance! I just want you to forgive him. Is that too much to ask?"

"Mom!" Gwen exploded, "I can't forgive a man who has practically beat me all those times. *You're* the one who needs to be understanding. You don't know Dad the way I do!"

"All right, Gwen, maybe Dad's hard to live with, but someone has to make the first move to change things around here. All I'm asking is that you do your part."

Gwen's face was red, she was so exasperated. "Mom, I hate it when you tell me that. Who's the adult around here? You and Dad are supposed to be! So why do I have to be the one to do all the changing?" She thought a brief second about what she had just said and blurted out, "No! I'm not going to do it. If you want me to forgive Dad, tell him he's got to give me a reason to. Until he does, I'm through with him!"

• • • •

Was this mother listening to her daughter—listening beyond the words to the emotions and meaning behind the words? Let's look at the same dialogue and see how a listening response can bring about a different ending. The conversation takes a different route when the mother shows understanding.

Situation: Looking Gwen squarely in the eye to attract her daughter's attention, Ellie said, "Gwen, I'm bothered by the way you and Dad haven't been getting along. It hurts me to see you argue as you do. Maybe it's because my dad died when I was thirteen, but I want you to have the relationship with your dad that I couldn't have."

Gwen shook her head back and forth, afraid that this would be another one of *those* conversations. "Mom, you just don't understand. I know you didn't have your father around for too long. But did he treat you the way

Dad treats me? I doubt it. Your dad didn't hit you and then call it a spanking, did he? How can I act as if I love him? I can't do that. Too much has gone on between Dad and me. You've just got to give me time."

A relaxed expression covered Ellie's face. She wished she did not have to hear Gwen talk as she did, but she knew that her daughter had been hurt by the frequent punishments her father doled out. "Dad's rough on you. You'd like it more than anything if he would take it easier on you."

Sensing that it was safer to dip deeper into her emotional bucket, Gwen probed, "Mom, why is he that way? Doesn't he see what he's doing to me?"

Ellie cocked her head sideways, silently gesturing that Gwen's question could not be easily answered. "You wish he did. You'd probably like to tell him exactly what you think. I'm sure that's a scary thought."

Gwen raised her eyebrows. "Tell Dad what I think? Ha! That'll be the day."

"I just wish that you could forgive your dad and start fresh with him."

"Forgive him? I can't forgive a man who has practically beat me all those times. I just can't do it."

"Maybe that's too much for you to do right now. You probably think he needs to reach out to you first. That would make it easier for you to do your part to heal the relationship."

"I don't think that'll ever happen, Mom. You know Dad. He's too proud."

Nodding her head to signal that she knew exactly what Gwen meant, Ellie added, "Pride does funny things to a man. It keeps him from admitting his mistakes." Pausing, Ellie thought while Gwen sighed deeply. Then touching Gwen's forearm, she said, "Teenagers can get hung up with their pride too. So can mothers. Maybe it's not the way it should be, but if you do the things you know are right, who knows? Maybe you'll end up influencing your father."

"Huh. I doubt it. I wish . . . but you know Dad."

Gently squeezing Gwen's arm, Ellie added, "I also know you, and I've got tons of respect for a young person who can see things as clearly as you do."

Gwen nodded her head. She felt better after talking to her mom. She knew she had one ally in the home.

• • • •

Analysis: In the initial dialogue, Ellie's emphasis was on making an important point. She was convinced that if things were to change between Gwen and her father, Gwen would have to initiate it. As unfair as that seemed to Gwen, Ellie practically begged Gwen to consider forgiving her father. Feeling misunderstood, Gwen ended up attacking her mom. She left the conversation frustrated. And the chances of developing a forgiving attitude toward her dad were slimmer than when the conversation began.

In the second conversation, Ellie acknowledged that Gwen's feelings toward her dad were valid. Gwen instinctively knew that her mother wanted things to be better between the two, so Ellie refused to force her beliefs on the girl. Instead, she stated aloud the feelings she thought her daughter was experiencing. Gwen was more open when her mother suggested that Gwen do her part to heal family relations. By listening to her daughter, Ellie increased her influence over the girl.

UNDERSTANDING DEFUSES DISAGREEMENTS

Disagreements will arise in families. As we saw in chapter 6, some families may have well-developed argumentative patterns. Parents are too frequently placed in the awkward position of having to make unpopular decisions even though they fully understand their child's opposition. Or husbands and wives may be compelled to act one way, knowing that their spouse has a different perspective.

A predictable pattern emerges when family members disagree with one another. It goes something like this:

- Two family members have differing points of view about a subject. If a decision is made, one person will surely "lose."
- After expressing that he understands the other person, the first will proceed to try to convince the other of his viewpoint.
- The second family member will reject the first's argument. In turn, he will try to force acceptance of his opinion.
- Like a Ferris wheel, the two persons go round and round, never reaching an agreement. A decision is ultimately settled upon, leaving one or both persons dissatisfied.
- The "defeated" family member will look for some way to salvage a victory from the dispute. Even if that victory simply means making the other person as mad as he is, he will do what he can to recover some sense of triumph.

There is a right way and a wrong way for family members to disagree. Here is a comparison of the two:

Right Way	Wrong Way
accepts the inevitability of disagreements	is upset over disagreements
gives others the right to thoughts/feelings	forces personal thoughts/feelings
listens to understand	listens to argue
asks fair questions	asks loaded questions
sticks to the subject	wanders; exaggerates
seeks what is fair and right	seeks revenge
waits for proper time to state opinion	disregards timing; spouts off
willing to compromise	wants to win

Note how a wife used her understanding of her husband to make the most of a marital disagreement:

Situation: A discipline problem erupted in the family. Dad handled the situation by talking roughly to the children and then punishing them harshly. His wife would have managed things differently. Rather than chastise her husband for his stern ways, the wife waited until the emotional dust had settled and approached her husband. "You were really mad at the kids earlier," was all she said. She could have said more about the way he had damaged family relations with his verbal

sledgehammer, but refrained. Her intent was to be of
support to her husband.

Sensing the absence of his wife's judgment, even
though he realized she disagreed, the husband talked
about his frustrations. "I was so mad at those two, I
thought I could spit real venom."

"I know. You were *really* mad. It's been some time since
I've seen you that angry. It scared me—the kids too."

"Yeah, well, I meant to scare them. I've had it with
the way they ignore the rules around here." He paused.
His wife said nothing, but raised her eyebrows, trigger-
ing a thought in the man's mind. "Maybe I scared them
too much."

"Maybe. I don't think they knew how to react. But
then, maybe you were so mad, you didn't care how
they felt."

"I know. I hate it when I act like that. I get mad and
say things I shouldn't, but then I feel bad about it later.
I probably ought to apologize to the kids."

"They'd like that. Probably do you good too. I know
you want things to get back to normal around here. We
all do. Nothing's worse than having all this tension fill
the house."

"Tell me about it. I don't want the kids to be frightened of me. I want them to respect me, though. And I
don't want you to be mad. I hate it when we're mad at
each other."

"This whole ordeal turned out worse than any of us
expected, didn't it?"

"Got any ideas of what to do?"

Analysis: Throughout their dialogue the wife maintained a listening stance, avoiding criticism. At the end

of the conversation, the husband felt relieved of his stress. He independently concluded that he needed to repair the damage he had caused the children. He asked his wife what he should do to make things right with the kids.

Had this wife become involved in the brawl between her husband and children, she would have become a part of the problem and could not have encouraged change. Her show of understanding helped her spouse to look honestly at himself in a way he would not have done otherwise. She stifled the urge to voice her disagreement. He knew exactly what she thought. By encouraging him to express his frustrations, she increased the likelihood that he would make the very adjustments she would have suggested. She even established herself as a valuable resource to use for making tough decisions.

USE COMMUNICATION TO RESPOND TO NEEDS

Remember that the goal we are working toward in this book is understanding our family members' behavior so that we can respond and meet their real needs. Responding is not a simple process. Responses may be verbal acts such as discussing, griping, lecturing, rephrasing, questioning, or yelling. A response may be a physical act such as touching, nodding, embracing, pointing, pouting, or any of an endless range of behaviors. Our entire body may be engaged, as when we cry, intimidate, ignore, threaten, sympathize, or caress.

The desired result of an effective response is to link two people to each other. That closeness may be emotional, physical, spiritual, or intellectual. Note in the following family dialogues how effective responses bring family members together.

> **Child:** I'm so dumb. I know that's why the other kids don't like me.

> **Parent:** It hurts to see all the other kids having fun when you feel that you're not a part of it.

Comment: The child probably has much more to say than this initial offering. Most kids start with an attention-getting statement as a way to signal a desire to talk about a personal need. For that matter, so do adults. The response given lets the child know that the full meaning of what has been said has been accepted. It uncovers underlying feelings. The parent has neatly paved the way for further conversation, either now or later. Note that the parent made no attempt to solve the problem. That job can be done after the task of affirmation has been completed.

••••

> **Wife:** I wish we could do something about the kids and their mess. There's junk all over the house. Their popcorn bowls are in the living room. Dirty clothes are anywhere except the clothes hamper. Mud is all over the kitchen floor. You can't see the carpet in their bedrooms because of their piles of clothes.

> **Husband:** It's as if you've been taken for granted. Keeping the house clean is a never-ending job. I'll do what I can to help. Maybe we can let the kids

know that we need some cooperation from them too.

Comment: This husband has taken his wife seriously. He accurately perceives her complaint as a subtle request for help and becomes tangibly involved by pledging to do what he can to make things better. This understanding response makes the wife more likely to view the husband as a teammate rather than an adversary.

• • • •

Mother: It's very important that we leave on time. I'm in charge of the meeting and want to be there early to get things organized.

Child: (nods and later arrives at the front door, ready and on time)

Comment: Although no words were exchanged, this child responded to the mother through behavior. Without words, the child communicated, "I respect your need for promptness and will honor your request." The mother should reinforce the positive behavior by commending the child, indicating how important his or her cooperation is to her. Parental acknowledgment of positive nonverbal responses increases the likelihood of their repetition.

• • • •

Teenager: I'm just about ready to give up. I've tried everything I can think of to be nice to Heather, but she just won't give me a chance. She acts nice, but

I'm not sure she really means it. I want to know if she wants to be close to me or not.

Parent: You may be defeating yourself with those thoughts. You've had some success with her, but you want complete success to come all at once. Relationships don't develop overnight. It takes time. You're doing the right things, but you need patience.

Comment: This response is risky and is one that will be effective only if there is already a strong rapport between parent and child. The parent is offering a different point of view and is giving direction. Note that the parent offers help in a positive, hopeful tone yet sends a message that appropriate follow-up is the teenager's responsibility. The effectiveness of this response will not be seen immediately. Confrontational responses like this should be used sparingly and only after it is apparent that the other family member feels understood.

• • • •

Like the act of listening, the act of responding calls for personal preparation. The intent of a response should be to stimulate the relationship. As you prepare to respond to family members, be aware of your own reaction to these questions:

- Do I show my personal concern, or do I give too much emphasis to action?
- Can I keep the focus on the other person's needs, or do I stress my own needs?

- Do I show my personal views too much or not enough?
- Am I good at showing flexibility as the situation requires?
- Does my personal agenda match the needs of the entire family?
- How comfortable am I with confrontation? Do I use it effectively?
- What does my response style say about me? Am I brazen, compassionate, zealous, patient, understanding, or wishy-washy?
- Do I try too hard to push solutions onto family problems? Does my tendency help or hinder family progress?

BUILD AN ATMOSPHERE THAT PROMOTES COMMUNICATION

Parents set the tone for the family atmosphere. As you try to be an effective leader in your family, remember this principle: *Effective family leaders not only are emotionally healthy but also recognize that each member can bring something positive to the home.* Consider the impact of these family leaders on the home atmosphere:

- A husband works from twelve to fourteen hours a day and virtually refuses to take a day off. He says he is setting a good example for the children because he is showing the significance of a strong work ethic. His wife disagrees. She says he is conveying the importance of work over family. What time he spends at home, he and his wife argue about what his behavior communicates.
- A mother considers her only real obligation to be

her children. A totally devoted mother, she spends practically every waking moment engrossed in her children's activities. The kids used to enjoy all the attention. As they have grown older, they view their mother as something of a nuisance. It seems that she will not let them live a life of their own.

• A wife's first husband was abusive in every possible way. Compared to the torturous years she spent with him, her current husband is a "dream boat" even though he drinks heavily and has little to do with her children. Whenever people ask her why she refuses to demand that he fulfill a more fatherly role, she simply replies, "Honey, as long as he pays the bills and treats me decent, everything's all right. The kids and I can take care of ourselves."

• A father believes that his most important family duty is to instill respect in his children. He points to the fact that his children seldom misbehave at school, quickly obey his commands, and keep a shipshape house as proof that his methods work. He ignores the fact that his children feel oppressed and secretly cannot wait for the day they can leave home.

Each of these parents wields a strong influence—both positive and negative—on the home atmosphere. The atmosphere, in turn, impacts the family's ability to communicate. Both the parents' behavior and personalities impact the emotional health of the family. Obviously, no two parents or sets of parents are alike, but all parents can follow the same guidelines for setting a tone that leads to family wholeness. Parents should not attempt to be something they are not. We must be real.

LINKING UNDERSTANDING, ATMOSPHERE, AND COMMUNICATION

We have already discussed the most common complaint of family members: *You just don't understand me.* Indeed, feeling understood is one of the most gratifying sensations a person may experience. Without it, meaningful family life grinds to a halt. Children who feel misunderstood resort to misbehavior to communicate their true feelings, hoping somehow to get across their message. Spouses play verbal cat and mouse, chasing each other with words that beg for comprehension. A lack of understanding among family members is a root cause for many power struggles.

When family leaders show understanding in the home, the entire atmosphere changes. Listen to the comments made by family members who feel understood:

- "It's as if they became me while I was talking."
- "I wasn't told I shouldn't feel that way. They accepted my feelings."
- "I didn't have to keep repeating myself. They knew what I meant."
- "I started talking, and they listened. It felt so good that I kept on talking."
- "I couldn't believe they were so calm while I talked. It felt so comfortable."
- "For the first time I started to believe that I could understand myself."
- "They didn't say much, but I knew they felt what I felt. They wanted to hear more."

Understanding is a gift. Without it, family members feel empty. Yet understanding does not necessarily equal agreement. Parents can understand why a child misbe-haved even though they wish the youngster had shown better judgment. Or a wife may see things as her hus-band does, though she would have called the shots differ-ently. Fearing that understanding will suggest agreement is what prevents most parents from meeting their family members' needs. But note how understanding boosts the family's morale in spite of disagreement:

> *Husband:* I've been home fifteen minutes, and already I've had to settle two fights between the kids. I know you're thinking that I need to hold my temper. If I could just have a little time to unwind, maybe I could be a little more patient.

> *Wife:* Wouldn't it be nice to come home to a calm, quiet house where you could kick off your shoes, read the paper, and relax before you had to deal with the kids?

Comment: Even though this wife may have agreed that her husband needed more patience, she realized that an understanding response would soothe her husband more than a defensive reaction. Her influence over her husband was much stronger by virtue of her concern for his needs. The children also benefited by her quiet-ing effect over their short-tempered dad.

• • • •

> *Son:* If I don't make a 97 on tomorrow's test, I'll have a D in English. How am I supposed to do that? The highest I've made all year is an 88!

> *Mother:* You've never gotten a D before, have you? That would hurt.

Comment: The child is fully aware that his parents want to see higher grades than what he is likely to make. No need to mention that fact. By focusing on his concern, the parent is much more likely to see her child hit the books than if she harped on his past failures.

• • • •

To create an understanding tone in the home, parents must dare to delve into the other person's world. By momentarily thinking as the other family member thinks, the parent sends this message: It is important to me that you know I am on your side. If I show you that I understand you, we can move forward together.

Trivial as it may seem, the point must be made that respect is a key component to a healthy home atmosphere. That seems like a simple concept, but it is difficult to achieve. Respect for individual differences involves acceptance of such traits as irritability, sensitivity, self-centeredness, and inflexibility. Family leaders show respect by refraining from wrestling emotional control from other family members. Note the contrasting interpretations given to the responses in the following conversations:

> *Teenager:* Dad thinks he knows everything. I can't say anything to him without him giving his opinion. He tries to tell me how to think, how to feel, how to act. I can't stand the way he pushes himself on me.

Mother's ineffective response: Don't you think Dad's just trying to help you? Maybe he sounds like he's pushy, but he's really not. I know he's just trying to show you he loves you.

Teenager's interpretation: It's useless to talk to my mom. She always takes Dad's side.

Mother's helpful response: It hurts to feel that Dad doesn't understand you any better than it seems he does.

Teenager's interpretation: I can trust my feelings to my mother. She respects what I feel, even though I know she wishes it were different between me and Dad.

••••

Wife: I wish you wouldn't sit in front of the television all night. The kids and I need you.

Husband's ineffective response: Don't tell me I sit in front of the television too much. Who's idea was it to watch this show? I'd rather be watching football.

Wife's interpretation: He's hopeless. He refuses to admit that maybe I'm right and he's wrong.

Husband's helpful response: I park in front of the television, and it's hard for me to get away. I know that irritates you.

> **Wife's interpretation:** Maybe he's willing to talk with
> me about ways we can resolve this problem.

• • • •

Showing respect to family members does not absolve
the adult from taking necessary action. Even though a
mother respects her child's right to be mad at his
father, she still may state that she will not tolerate dis-
courteous behavior. Or a wife may still face a marital
showdown over whether the television stays on or
goes off. Respect suggests that in spite of individual
differences, one family member will not deny the
other the right to feel as he or she does. As this quality
is shown, family members are more likely to respond
openly to one another. Hidden struggles for emotional
control can be avoided. An atmosphere for growth is
deepened.

BUILD FAMILY COMMUNICATION THROUGH TRUST
One of the most painful experiences for any child,
adolescent, or adult is to admit to personal failure. Having to admit that life has thrown an unhittable curve-
ball can be embarrassing, demoralizing, annoying, or
maddening. None of us likes to concede defeat. Think
of the many times you have heard phrases such as, "I
don't want to talk about it" or "I hate to admit this,
but . . ." or "You won't believe me when I tell you" or
"I didn't tell you because I didn't want to hurt you."
Such language suggests that it is hard to trust certain
thoughts and feelings to anyone else.

And it is.

Ask a child or spouse why he or she opened up to
family members, though, and the likely response will

be, "I can trust them." Trust suggests security. When trust is present, there is a sense of faith in the home environment, an optimism that the home is a sanctuary where growth occurs. Conversely, in an atmosphere of mistrust such things as suspicion, withdrawal, fearfulness, or anxiety may grow. Note how trusting the father is in the following dialogue with his son.

> *Father:* I had a talk with Melissa's mom earlier today.

> *Gil (nervous but trying to hide it):* Oh yeah? About what?

> *Father:* You probably don't have to guess what we talked about. *(pause)* She told me about what happened at her house Saturday night.

> *Gil (head hanging):* Oh.

> *Father:* Here's what I know. She said that Melissa was supposed to be home at eleven o'clock. You had her home by then, and it seemed that everything was all right. But about thirty minutes later she went to Melissa's bedroom to check on her and found you hiding behind the bed. Is that much accurate?

> *Gil:* I guess.

> *Father:* I'd like to hear things from your view. Tell me what you can.

Gil: There's not much to say. I took her home, waited a few minutes, and then she let me in the bedroom window. It's pretty much what her mother told you.

Father: I know you feel uncomfortable talking about this. Getting caught breaking a rule like that is pretty humiliating. *(Gil still looking down)* I'm sure you can guess what Melissa's parents are most concerned about.

Gil: What?

Father: Virtually any parent would assume that something sexual was about to happen. Teenagers are prone to things like that.

Gil: Honest, Dad. It wasn't that way. Nothing happened. We were just stupid, that's all. I wish I had never done that.

Father: I'm sure if you could turn back the hands of time and change things, you would do things differently. We all feel foolish when we've been caught in a big mistake. *(pause)* Melissa's parents are pretty upset with you. And I'm sure they're not real happy with Melissa either.

Gil: What's going to happen?

Father: I can't say what her parents will do. I can guess that you and Melissa won't be seeing each other as much as you have been—at least not for a while. I haven't decided yet what I'm going to do. I need to think about it some more.

Gil: Does Mom know?

Father: Yes, she knows. She wanted to join me when we talked, but I thought that maybe you might feel overwhelmed if both of us pounced on you. She plans to discuss things with you later. We're both hurt, but I know that you're not feeling good about this whole thing either.

• • • •

As this conversation wound down, Gil was able to focus on his own irresponsibility. His father did not pull him into a fight. The tone this dad set said, *You can trust me to keep your honor intact even though I disagree with what you have done.* That done, Gil could more easily conclude that he was wrong and needed to make things right again between himself and others.

Showing trust in the home involves

- refusing to condemn a family member who has acted wrongly (pardon)
- showing love even in the presence of personal failure (grace)
- believing that the child is basically good in spite of his or her errors (faith)
- displaying optimism for the future (hope)
- administering punishment in a respectful manner (honor)
- refusing to hold a grudge for past mistakes (forgiveness)

A home atmosphere that satisfies these emotional needs fosters trust. Children trust their parents to keep their best interests at heart when decisions are made. Children know that even though they will be held accountable for misdeeds, they will not be punished to the point of frustration. They will grow to believe that they can be optimistic about the future and that they can have faith in their parents' leadership.

Family life may be described as a series of tests. Children test their parents to determine if their world is safe, understanding, respectful, and trustworthy. These traits may never be permanently achieved in a home because life continually tests the family's resolve to develop a positive home atmosphere. But the persistent efforts of parents can lead the family to maturity in spite of life's challenges. A climate that encourages growth can keep the family moving beyond temporary setbacks.

Summary: Effective family communication is one of the most important building blocks parents use to set the tone for family growth. Listening beyond the spoken words helps family members hear the real message behind the spoken one. When families commit themselves to understanding each other, trust grows.

The second building block parents offer to their family's growth is the strength of their marriage. The next chapter will examine how a strong marriage contributes to a strong family.

1. I mentioned in an earlier chapter that my favorite biblical passage is John 8:1-11. In this poignant story, we see how Jesus sets a tone that steers a wayward woman toward emotional healing. The qualities Jesus shows this woman can be applied in any relationship, especially in the home. Read this story together as a family and respond to these questions:

- What were the woman's emotions as she was thrown before Jesus? What did she assume he was feeling about her?
- How did Jesus change the atmosphere from one of condemnation to one of forgiveness?
- What about Jesus' reaction might have moved the woman toward change?
- In what ways do family members try to force their judgment on one another, only to see their efforts backfire?
- Is it better that parents show understanding, respect, and trust in their children rather than punish them? Can both be accomplished at the same time? How?

2. Pick a time when you are around your family for an extended time. Take note of your response style and its effects on the family. Afterward rate yourself on a scale of 1 to 5 on the following items (1 = always,

2 = frequently, 3 = sometimes, 4 = hardly ever, 5 = never).
Be nakedly honest with yourself. Use your ratings as a
tool for personal growth.

- I make good eye contact when I communicate
  with others.
- I show patience when a problem arises.
- My nonverbal gestures match the words I use.
- My posture suggests that I am alert and inter-
  ested in others.
- I think first, then speak rather than speak first,
  then think.
- My eyes suggest friendliness.
- I use physical touch effectively.
- The volume of my voice is just about right.
- I speak in terms others understand.
- When I offer my opinion, I can say it in one
  minute or less.
- I make comments that stimulate further com-
  ment or discussion.
- I feel comfortable talking about feelings and
  emotions.

3. Think back to the most recent disagreement you had
with a family member. Critique yourself by asking the
following questions. If you feel bold, ask that family
member to critique you as well.

- Did I understand what that family member was
  thinking? Did the person think I understood him
  or her?
- Did we become hooked in a power struggle?
  Who won? Who lost? Was it worth the trouble?

- Did I take the disagreement personally? What was the effect of the disagreement on me?
- Did I get hung up on the principle of the matter and act without regard for the other person's feelings?
- Did I try too hard to force my opinions on the family member? Did I succeed?
- Which comments should I have smothered? What should I have said?
- What is likely to happen the next time a similar situation occurs? What do I plan to do differently?
- What comments that the family member said to me or about me do I need to think about and consider seriously?

CHAPTER TWELVE

Strong Marriage, Strong Family

HAVING children does not strengthen a marriage.

There. I said it. Might as well dispel that myth right away.

Using children to pull a family together is neither fair to the kids nor the right path for a husband and wife to build a strong family. If the truth were known, having children puts a strain on most marriages. Not that all stress is bad for a marriage, but the day-to-day requirements of parenthood can test the strength of any marriage.

The marital relationship is the cornerstone of all other family relationships. Think of all the verbal evidence family members offer to confirm this truth. Listen as the following family members speak:

> **Unruly young boy:** My daddy talks bad to my mama. Then he talks bad to me. But I can't talk

that way. It's against the rules. I'm in trouble all the time for breaking the rules.

Teenager: This place is so depressing! You wonder why I'm mad all the time? Just look at what goes on around here! Mom and Dad can't agree on anything. Nobody seems to know what anybody else is doing. If anything gets done, it's because *I* do it. When my sister says anything to my brother, he tattles, and then Mom and Dad get mad about that because they say they're sick of all the junk that happens in our house. Get me outta here!

Wife: I hoped things would get better when we divorced. I thought the children would be relieved because they wouldn't have to listen to me and their father fight anymore. I know they're glad about that, but now that he's gone, it's like they forgot what a louse he really is. They blame *me* for everything that's wrong in our family. As if I can do anything about how awful things were before the divorce!

Father: Nobody talks in our family. It's as if we all have these private secrets. My wife tries to get me to open up to her, but I'm not about to. She'll tell the kids my business.

Throughout this book, I have referred to family leadership as a joint effort between husband and wife, but I would like to give clarification to that image. It is hard to categorize the duties of the father as opposed to the mother, though some have made attempts to do just that. It seems more reasonable to allow for flexibility in slicing up family duties. Certain tasks tend to be designated as motherly duties, while other chores are assigned to the father. For example, mothers may prepare meals and do the laundry, while fathers may mow the lawn and do car maintenance.

A marriage relationship that views family responsibilities as joint obligations is one that runs smoothly. Husbands and wives should "cross train" so that each can take care of the other's most common tasks. Each spouse should know how to do such things as change diapers, shop for groceries, mow the lawn, prepare the children's baths, wash clothes, sweep the patio, barbecue on the grill, have the car oil changed, or talk to the kids' teachers. Let's replace the words *that's your job* in *The Marital Book of Commonly Used Phrases* with the words *it's our job.*

As family leaders, schedule regular discussions about such family-management topics as child-rearing practices, money issues, scheduling, family gatherings, or future plans. Discuss these issues when your children are not around and when your emotions are under control. Make the goal of your discussions unity. The family needs leaders who are moving in the same direction. When disagreements arise, refuse to be dogmatic. Although being opinionated, closed minded, domineering, emphatic, or aggressive may work in some businesses, it does not work in the home.

Know yourself inside out. While all couples can recite the importance of being friends with one another, too many forget that they need to be friends with themselves too. Talk to your spouse regularly about new personal insights you have gained. If you simply cannot see anything new about yourself, ask your spouse to reflect what he or she sees. Or look at what you already know about yourself in a different light. Be convinced that blunt honesty with yourself is the ticket to growth. Never quit growing as a person or as a couple.

Give each other emotional "paychecks" in front of the children. Openly compliment one another for a job well done. Doing so buoys up the kids' belief that both of you deserve their respect. Remember that compliments are far more effective tools than criticism in helping others to change.

Try to help family members feel valued and equal. Lining up family members from positions of superiority to inferiority serves only to make the family look like a totem pole. And totem poles are made of figures wearing masks. When each family member feels equally valued, masks are thrown away. Everyone contributes proportionately to the family.

LEARN EFFECTIVE COMMUNICATION

Perhaps the most common complaint of married couples is that of failed communication. When couples can no longer express what they feel, the family atmosphere turns sour. There is often much fear beneath failed communication. When couples are honest about the collapse of their marital exchanges, they make statements such as the following. Listen for the fear beneath each comment.

- "If I say what I really think, I'll never hear the end of it."
- "I try to be open and honest, but when I do, I

feel put down. It's as if I'm being told to quit feeling the way I do. I can't!"
- "I don't want to talk to somebody who just tries to change my mind for me. I need help sorting out my feelings."
- "He thinks I'm going to push myself on him, so he won't listen. Then I feel that I have to be pushy just to get his attention."
- "Every time I admit to a mistake, my spouse makes me feel so small. Why talk?"
- "I try to talk, but when I do, she cuts me off. She wants to give her side. I usually just say, 'Forget it.'"
- "I honestly don't think he cares what I feel. As long as I give him the basics, he's satisfied. He's so self-centered, he doesn't think about me."

Healthy communication between a couple drives away fear. As you think about your marriage relationship, keep in mind this simple truth: The facts of life are friendly. What do I mean by that?

- Mistakes are an inevitable part of life. When I learn to live with them, I will find that many will be spontaneously corrected.
- It is not my obligation to fix everything that is wrong in a relationship. Time and my patience have a way of seeing the best of life rise to the top.
- When I try to force change, I find myself in power struggles. When I make myself available as a supportive helper, things improve.
- There is a meaning and purpose to everything we

do. When I take the time to uncover hidden messages, I can give a well-informed response.
- Some of the best-laid plans simply do not work out. Alternatives are always available.
- Every rule has its exceptions.
- No matter how painful a situation is, God can use it for good.

If we view the facts of married life as ultimately friendly, we will not be afraid to discuss any topic. Drawing from the ideas already presented about listening and responding, think about these guidelines for healthy marital communication.

The power of communication lies in the willingness to listen. Effective communicators do not simply say what they think others want to hear. They hone in on what others feel. They sense their spouse's emotional heartbeat. When your spouse talks, try to visualize what he or she is saying and feeling. Draw each other out. Conversations peppered with phrases such as "What do you think," "I'd like your input," or "Help me sort this out" lead to unity and cooperation.

Don't be afraid of mistakes: They provide a stepping-stone for improvement. By accepting them, talking about them, and learning from them, you can move forward in your marriage. Repeated mistakes mark the need for repeated walks down the same road. Each time a couple travels that way, they see something new about themselves. Remember that *being right* is not nearly as important as *making a relationship right*. At times the right thing is to surrender. Someone has said, "When a spouse turns the other cheek, the sting in the hand hurts worse than the sting on the cheek."

Timing is everything. Before you blurt out your recent thoughts to your spouse, remember that there is a time and place for every thought. The worst time is when emotions run high. Make sure your communication is not disturbed by the static of tensions that rose earlier in your day, a screaming infant, or a blaring television program.

TAKE TIME OUT FOR FUN

Remember the fun you had when you first married each other?

Like most couples, you probably worked hard at getting your relationship off to a good start. You spent lots of time together—talking, planning, dreaming. You planned activities just because you liked being together. When you and your spouse disagreed, you often set aside your personal desire in favor of your spouse's preferences, or you gave in because doing so would keep the relationship going. Every now and then, you splurged to do something special for the other. You bragged about the other to friends or family. And you showed affection frequently and unashamedly.

Even after long years of marriage, each of these elements can find its way back into a relationship. Breathing refreshing life into a union takes commitment, just as it did when the two of you were first married. Here are some suggestions for injecting life into your marriage:

- Nothing catches another person's attention like the unexpected. Surprise your spouse with any one of these gestures: do the dishes every night for a month; let someone else sit in "your" chair; go last in line; offer a public prayer; let the other person decide; wear something different; or warm your spouse's side of the bed just before bedtime. Refuse to become a slave to habit. Change with life.

- Get the kids to help you plan and carry out a surprise activity. Let the whole family know that you enjoy doing things for your spouse.
- Return to a place that has sentimental attachment for the two of you. Even if it is a place you visit regularly, stop and talk about the good times you had together in the place.
- Send regular messages to your spouse to indicate that you carry thoughts of your relationship wherever you go. Whether you leave messages for each other on the answering machine, send friendship cards through the mail, or stick notes on the bathroom mirror, make an effort to keep saying thanks for being a friend.
- "Pinch-hit" when it is obvious that your spouse is weary, even if you are too. You will be surprised how quickly your spouse's strength is renewed.
- If you know of a need your in-laws have, do what you can to meet it. Showing love and care to your spouse's family blesses your spouse.
- Go out on a date with your spouse, at least once a month if possible. Send the message to both your spouse and your children that your marriage is that important.

Summary: One of the best investments in your family's growth is a strong marriage. When the pressures of kids' schedules and needs blunt the edge of your time together, take time to sharpen your marriage. Your whole family will benefit.

1. As we end this final chapter on family relationships, take a nostalgic look around your home. Let your children help you sort through old clothes, toys, games, books, or papers. Talk about events that were associated with these items.

2. If you have family photos or videos available, get them out and look through them as a family. Show the children pictures of you and your spouse before you married. Tell them stories about life before you were married. The purpose of these dialogues should be to give your children a glimpse of their heritage.

3. Make it your intent to bring some life into your marriage. Choose from any of the following activities to increase the positive interactions between you and your spouse. If you want to let the kids witness your acts of kindness toward each other, do so. They'll benefit from seeing you and your spouse enjoying one another.

- Spend an hour reminiscing. Talk about when you first began to date. Recall your first impressions of each other and how they have changed through the years. Talk about the good things that have resulted from adverse situations.
- On a given day, switch roles. The wife should take care of the household chores that the hus-

band normally does, and the husband should take his wife's. Offer no advice to your spouse on how things should be done. Later, talk about the impact this experiment had on your view of your spouse. Use this cross-training exercise as a starting point for creating a partnership between the two of you.

- Buy your spouse a present. You need no other reason than to show that you care.
- Actively seek an opportunity to brag about your spouse in front of other people. It's not necessary to be showy. Just say things to others to let your spouse know you believe in him or her.
- Select an hour during the coming week, and silently count the number of positive statements and gestures you make toward your spouse. On the next night, double that number during a given hour.

About the Author

Wm. Lee Carter *is a licensed psychologist in private practice in Waco, Texas. He works with children, adolescents, and their families in inpatient, outpatient, and residential-treatment settings. Lee and his wife, Julie, are the parents of three daughters, Emily, Sarah, and Mary. His family often serves as his first editorial board for his writing.*

Other books by Dr. Wm. Lee Carter

- *The Parent-Child Connection*

- *KidThink: Understand How Your Kids Think and Use It to Help Them*

- *Family Cycles: How Understanding the Way You Were Raised Will Make You a Better Parent*

- *The Angry Teenager: Why Teens Get So Angry and How Parents Can Help Them Grow through It*

- *Carry Me Home (a novel)*